craft **workshop**

enamel

craft **workshop**

enamel

The art of enamelling in 25 beautiful projects

Denise Palmer

Photography by Peter Williams

southwater

738.4

This edition is published by Southwater

Southwater is an imprint of Anness Publishing Ltd
Hermes House, 88–89 Blackfriars Road, London SE1 8HA
tel. 020 7401 2077; fax 020 7633 9499
www.southwaterbooks.com; info@anness.com

© Anness Publishing Ltd 1998, 2003

UK agent: The Manning Partnership Ltd,
6 The Old Dairy, Melcombe Road, Bath BA2 3LR;
tel. 01225 478444; fax 01225 478440;
sales@manning-partnership.co.uk

UK distributor: Grantham Book Services Ltd,
Isaac Newton Way, Alma Park Industrial Estate,
Grantham, Lincs NG31 9SD; tel. 01476 541080;
fax 01476 541061; orders@gbs.tbs-ltd.co.uk

North American agent/distributor: National Book Network,
4501 Forbes Boulevard, Suite 200, Lanham, MD 20706;
tel. 301 459 3366; fax 301 429 5746; www.nbnbooks.com

Australian agent/distributor: Pan Macmillan Australia,
Level 18, St Martins Tower, 31 Market St, Sydney, NSW 2000;
tel. 1300 135 113; fax 1300 135 103;
customer.service@macmillan.com.au

New Zealand agent/distributor: David Bateman Ltd,
30 Tarndale Grove, Off Bush Road, Albany, Auckland;
tel. (09) 415 7664; fax (09) 415 8892

A CIP catalogue record for this book is available from the British
Library.

Publisher: Joanna Lorenz
Senior Editor: Cathy Marriott
Designer: Lilian Lindblom
Photographer: Peter Williams
Step-by-step Photographer: Rodney Forte
Stylist: Georgina Rhodes
Illustrators: Madeleine David and Vana Haggerty

Previously published as New Crafts: Enamelling

10 9 8 7 6 5 4 3 2 1

Acknowledgements
The publishers would like to thank the contributors for the following projects and text: Sarah Wilson – Materials, Equipment and Basic techniques (pages 18–27), Striped necklace (pages
42–4), Shield earrings (pages 53–5), Reptilian ring (pages 79–81), Wave brooch (pages 90–3); Ruth Rushby – Bird pin (pages 40–1), Gold foil beads (pages 58–60), Star patterned box lid
(pages 66–8), Cloisonné brooch (pages 69–71), Triangular pendant (pages 76–8), Cloisonné earrings (pages 84–6); Alex Raphael – Multicoloured buttons (pages 48–9), Abstract art
keyring (pages 56–7), Cloisonné bowl (pages 61–3), Plique-à-jour bowl (pages 72–3), Moon bowl (pages 87–9); Jane Moore – Stargazer earrings (pages 34–6), Pet brooch (pages 50–2),
Banded ring (pages 64–5), Fishy cufflinks (pages 74–5), Flower pendant (pages 82–3); Denise Palmer – Door plaque (pages 30–1), Night and day clock face (pages 45–7); Lisa Hamilton –
Fleur-de-lis bookmark (pages 28–9), Napkin rings (pages 37–9); Tina Cartledge – Geometric potstand (pages 32–3). Thank you also to Gudde at Camden Workshops for help and advice.

Publisher's Note
The author and publishers have made every effort to ensure that all the instructions in this book are accurate and safe, and therefore
cannot accept liability for any resulting injury, damage or loss to persons or property however it may arise.

CONTENTS

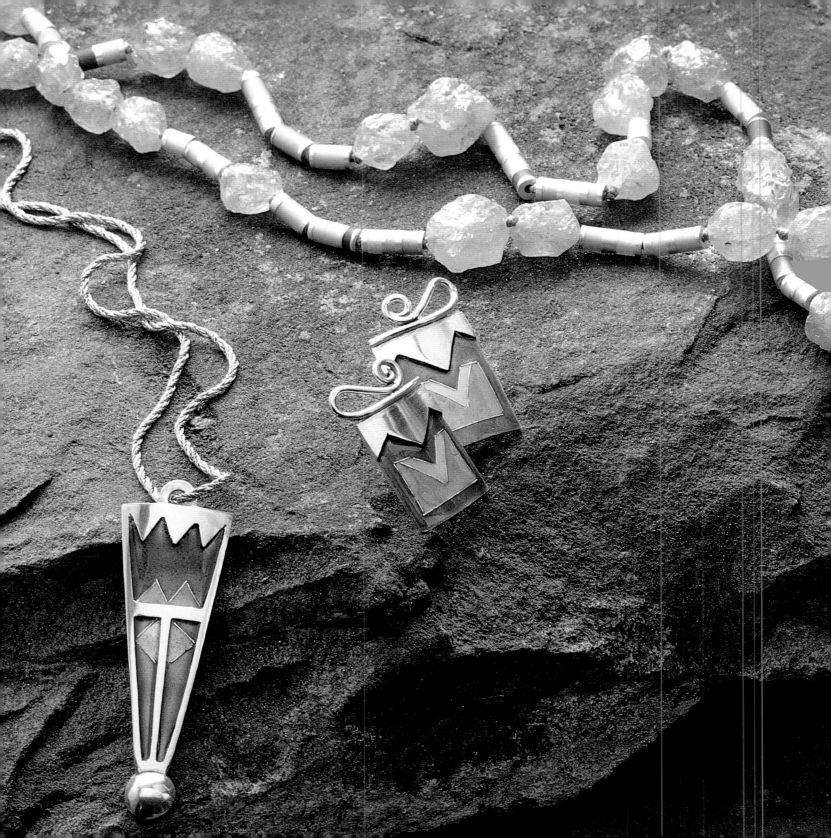

INTRODUCTION

ENAMEL IS A FORM OF GLASS, AND ENAMELLING IS THE PROCESS OF FUSING IT TO THE METAL WITH HEAT. THE CRAFT OF ENAMELLING HAS BEEN PRACTISED FOR CENTURIES AND DATES BACK TO 1400 BC. EARLY CIVILIZATIONS USED ENAMEL IN IMITATION OF PRECIOUS STONES. THE GREEKS AND ROMANS THEN DEVELOPED AND CONTINUED THE CRAFT OF ENAMELLING. SOME OF THE EARLIEST EXAMPLES OF ENAMEL CAN BE FOUND ON BUCKLES, SWORDS, COINS AND HELMETS FROM AS EARLY AS THE 5TH CENTURY BC. WORKING WITH METAL AND GLASS IS, FOR MANY, A CONTINUATION OF A BEAUTIFUL ART AND AN ANCIENT TRADITION. THIS ORIGINAL NEW BOOK CONTAINS ALL THE INFORMATION YOU WILL NEED TO PRODUCE 25 WONDERFUL PROJECTS. A COMPREHENSIVE TECHNIQUES SECTION SHOWS HOW TO PREPARE ENAMELS AND METAL, HOW TO APPLY ENAMELS TO THE METAL AND HOW TO FIRE A PIECE.

Left: Enamelling produces highly distinctive work, which is defined by a simplicity of design combined with rich colours.

THE HISTORY OF ENAMELLING

ENAMEL, WHICH IS A FORM OF GLASS, SHARES THAT MATERIAL'S QUALITIES OF BRILLIANCE AND PERMANENCE: THE COLOURS OF THE EARLIEST-KNOWN EXAMPLES OF ENAMELLING REMAIN AS RICH TODAY AS WHEN THEY WERE CREATED. ITS FLUIDITY OF APPLICATION, USING A VARIETY OF TECHNIQUES, HAS ALLOWED IT TO BE ADAPTED TO MANY DIFFERENT DECORATIVE TRADITIONS OVER AT LEAST 3000 YEARS. ALL THESE TECHNIQUES ARE STILL IN USE TODAY.

The technology of enamelling – using heat to fuse a vitreous material on to a metal base – has obscure beginnings, but it is thought to have originated in Europe. Although Egyptian craftsmen were skilled in the use of glass inlay, no examples of Egyptian enamel work have been found. One of the earliest surviving examples is a set of Mycenaean gold beads from around 1450 BC, enamelled in blue using the technique known as *champlevé*.

To contain molten enamel on a metal surface during firing, there are various methods of creating a raised border around it. In *champlevé* work, it is achieved by hammering, engraving, etching or stamping the surface to form recesses. The powdered enamel, mixed with water, is applied using a quill or brush and allowed to dry out before firing. Celtic craftsmen used *champlevé* enamelling on jewellery from around 400 BC and throughout the period of the Roman Empire. The Romans themselves, while preferring to decorate their jewellery with gemstones and cameos, used enamel to embellish medallions and larger objects.

From around the 6th century BC, Greek and Etruscan gold jewellery had been encrusted with filigree decorations of twisted wire. When enamel became popular during the Classical period, it was contained within these filigree designs, laid on the surface of the metal. In Europe, the Celts used metal strips instead of wires. For this technique, called *cloisonné*, the strips are attached to the surface at right angles to form small cells, or *cloisons*,

Above: This enamelled chest was made in Limoges in the 12–13th centuries. It uses champlevé *enamelling, a technique that allowed enamellers to produce pictures on copper.*

Left: This is a gold enamel cross from c. AD 1000. It is a good example of Byzantine enamelling as it contains pure, bright colours in finely beaten gold.

which contain the enamel. The enamel shrinks on firing, and when it has cooled its surface is lower than the outline. This form is known as Russian *cloisonné*, but in other traditions the enamel is topped up and re-fired so that the surface is flush with the metal strips.

From the 8th to the 12th centuries Byzantine *cloisonné* enamelling, distinguished by its use of pure colours in ornate designs on finely beaten gold, rose to great artistic heights. Examples of Byzantine *cloisonné* in the form of religious ornaments and icons found their way into churches all over Europe and had a far-reaching influence. A late Byzantine refinement of *cloisonné*, revived in the 19th century, is the fragile *plique-à-jour*. The cells of enamel are built up on a backing-plate, which is then removed, leaving a translucent surface like a miniature stained-glass window. Understandably, very few medieval examples of this technique have survived.

Plique-à-jour was made possible by the introduction of translucent enamel in the 13th century. It also allowed Italian metal-workers to display their virtuosity in the development of the *basse-taille* style. For this technique, the enamel is applied over a surface intricately chased with a pattern or picture. The varying thickness of the enamel results in subtle shading, and the colours gain brilliance from the shimmering silver or gold base.

Email en ronde bosse, a form of enamelling that the Greeks had first developed in the 3rd century BC, was again used during the Renaissance for jewellery and religious artefacts by artists such as Hans Holbein the Younger and Benvenuto Cellini. It involves layering enamel in high relief or applying it to sculpted shapes such as, for example, the gold mounts of a crystal reliquary. It is a characteristic embellishment of the self-consciously magnificent objects produced by craftsmen of the High Renaissance.

A radical development in the art of enamelling occurred during the Renaissance, when the mastery of firing at controlled temperatures enabled enamellers to produce pictures on copper. This technique was refined in France, specifically at Limoges, where *champlevé* enamelling had flourished since the 12th century. The earliest method involved

laying down a dark ground on to which opaque white enamel was applied, thinned in places to create shading. This monotone effect was known as *en grisaille*. Perfecting the art of painting in coloured enamels took much longer, but it was widely practised by the 17th century to decorate small, precious objects. The colours are laid down in many thin layers – perhaps 20 or more – each fired separately. Counter-enamelling (applying a layer or wash of enamel to the back of the piece for each layer on the front) prevents the metal from bending and cracking the enamel as it cools.

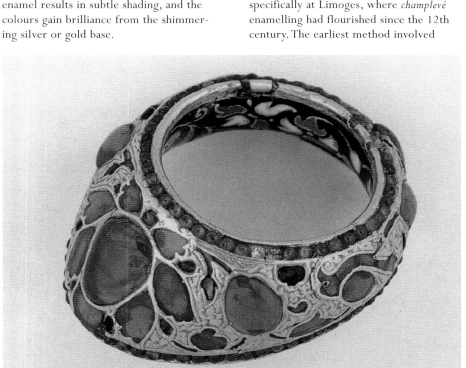

Above: This is the Royal Gold Cup of the Kings of England and France which was made in Paris c. 1380.

Left: A mogul ring from the early 17th century. It is made from gold, set with rubies and emeralds. It is enamelled on the inside only.

English watchmakers used painted enamel faces from the beginning of the 18th century, and over the next 50 years the fashion for painted enamel trinkets spread from France to England, where factories such as those in Battersea and Birmingham produced charming boxes, plaques and novelties. New industrial techniques, including more sophisticated kilns, meant that these could be mass-produced, using transfer-printed designs on a white enamel ground, which were then sometimes over-painted in coloured enamels or gilded.

The use of copper rather than gold, and the fact that printed designs could be quickly reproduced many times over, made enamel artefacts available to a much wider public. Little boxes with hinged lids were the most popular items, due to the 18th-century fashion for taking snuff. Many of the designs commemorated special dates or places, or were designed as presents or love tokens, bearing mottoes and expressions of affection. The decline in the fashion for snuff-taking also meant the end of the fashion for the boxes, about 100 years after it had begun.

In the late 17th century, European missionaries had taken painted enamels with them to Canton and Peking, where the technique was avidly copied. The Chinese had used *champlevé* enamelling since the 14th century, and sometimes combined it with *cloisonné*. Chinese *cloisonné* reached a peak of perfection during the 18th century and, though it has since declined in quality, it is still a major industry. In Japan, in contrast, a new school of *cloisonné* began in Kyoto at the end of the 19th century, producing naturalistic designs so fine they resembled painting.

Above: A plique à jour *bowl made by the Frenchman Fernard Thesmar in the late 19th century.* Plique à jour *creates the effect of a miniature stained-glass window.*

Left: This Viennese snuff box was made before 1793. It is made from gold and enamel. Cheaper versions were made from copper rather than gold and were very popular gentlemen's gifts in the 18th century.

Japanese enamellers also mastered the art of *plique-à-jour*, creating large pieces that were almost totally translucent.

In the West, commercial enamelling entered a new phase when it became possible to apply the material to iron in the 1850s. Applied to all household objects from saucepans to baths, enamelled metal became, and remains today, a highly functional and hard-wearing commodity.

Limoges painted enamels were revived in the 1840s, and later in the century the English artist Alexander Fisher produced enamels in the Renaissance style. Art Nouveau enamellers, including Louis Comfort Tiffany in New York and René Lalique in Paris, created free-flowing, organic patterns in which colours merged without hard outlines. The influence of Japanese enamelling was evident in the *plique-à-jour* jewellery of Lalique, combining delicate tracery with vivid colours.

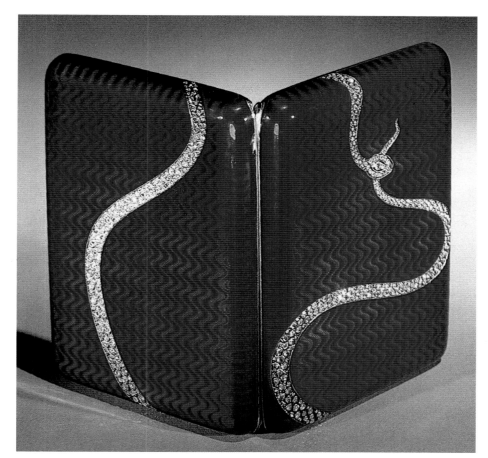

*Below: This is a 20th-century Japanese cloisonné vase.
It was made by Hiroki Oota (born 1912) and was exhibited
at the 1990 Limoges L'art de l'email Biennale
Internationale.*

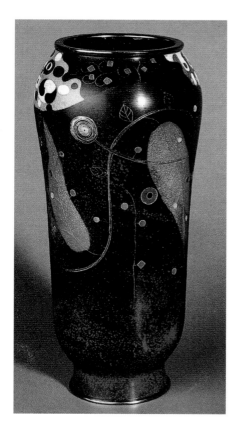

The 15th-century technique of *basse-taille* re-emerged centuries later with the invention of 'guilloché-moiré' engine-turning, which enabled fantastically intricate patterns to be created in the metal ground. *Basse-taille* enamelling reached its apogee in the work of Carl Fabergé, who took the European skills he had learned in Paris back to his Russian workshops and created unparalleled effects, notably on the famous series of Easter eggs he made for the Tsar and his family. These translucent enamels, often with painted motifs, have remained a familiar decoration on silver accessories such as picture frames, hairbrushes and coffee spoons for most of this century. In contrast, the uncompromising lines of Art Deco cried out for the strong, glossy colours of opaque enamel; *cloisonné* took on stark, geometric shapes in silver, black and red; and enamelling arrived firmly in the modern age.

Jewellery makers and other crafts-people have continued to find their own ways of using the various techniques of enamelling in 20th-century designs. A significant modern advance has been the introduction of the domestic-sized electric kiln, so that the craft has become accessible to anyone who wishes to pursue it.

GALLERY

ENAMELLISTS WORKING TODAY CONTINUE A TRADITION THAT DATES BACK CENTURIES, WORKING IN A WIDE RANGE OF PRECIOUS AND SEMI-PRECIOUS MATERIALS. WHILE THE TECHNIQUE IS OF OBVIOUS INTEREST TO JEWELLERY DESIGNERS, MANY CRAFTSPEOPLE USE IT TO EMBELLISH OTHER ARTEFACTS OR ENJOY THE MEDIUM FOR ITS OWN SAKE IN MORE ABSTRACT PIECES.

Above: PEN
The engraving beneath the transparent grey *champlevé* enamel provides a striking contrast with the clean, bold opaque enamel motifs.
PHIL BARNES

Above: CANDLESTICK
This is a silver and 18 carat gold candlestick with a photo-etched *champlevé* stem. The *champlevé* technique has created enamelled panels within which transparent colours and gold foil interplay.
TAMAR D. WINTER

Left: GOBLETS
The opaque enamel background of these silver and *cloisonné* goblets enhances the subtly shaded design. The snaking pattern, which flows through both goblets, provides a clever and unusual feature.
MAUREEN EDGAR

Above: NECKLACE
A stunning 'amulet and talisman' necklace of gold *cloisonné* enamel and silver beads. The beads illustrate a variety of ancient symbols. Different materials have also been used, including coral to depict life and death, amber, rose quartz, onyx, agate, cornelian crystal, garnet, amethyst, tourmaline, marble and shell.
ALEX RAPHAEL

Below: NECKLACE AND
ENAMELLED BOX
The necklace is made up
of silver enamelled beads
with pure gold foil
decoration. The unusual
cone-shaped box uses the
cloisonné enamel technique.
RUTH RUSHBY

Right: NECKLACE
The *champlevé* technique
was used on the central
bead of this necklace.
The remaining beads and
gold-rimmed oval are
made from quartz.
SARAH WILSON

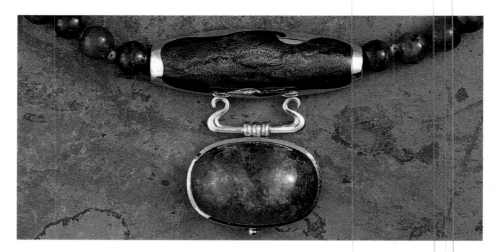

Above: 'OUT OF
BOUNDS'
A collage of enamel
has been applied to pre-
enamelled industrial steel
using sgraffito. Sgraffito
means that an applied layer
of enamel has been drawn
through using a paint-
brush, knife or scrubber
to reveal a fired undercoat.
When fired, the pattern
becomes the colour of the
enamel undercoat.
ELIZABETH TURRELL

Opposite: ORGANIC
JEWELLERY
These pieces have been
inspired by organic forms.
To construct the shapes in
silver, the enameller has
used spinning, hand raising
and stamping techniques.
The enamelled part of the
work consists of coiled
copper shim on to which
transparent enamel has
been fired. This binds
it together as well as
providing colour and
texture.
DENISE PALMER

Right: LAPEL
BROOCHES
Three lapel brooches that
would adorn any plain
jacket or coat. The designs
for these pieces have been
photo-etched on to silver
and then enamelled to give
a rich depth of colour.
JANE MOORE

Left: RINGS
The bright opaque enamel of these *champlevé* silver rings have been set with cabochan semi-precious stones. The fun, playful colours give the rings a very contemporary feel.
JOHN RICHARDSON

Below: GOBLET
The lacy design of this silver and enamel *plique-à-jour* goblet was formed from fine gold *cloisonné* ribbon wire painstakingly applied to a copper former. After enamelling, the copper is etched away to reveal the beautiful design.
ALEX RAPHAEL

Right: PLATE
This silver and *champlevé* plate has been set within a ziricote wooden bowl. The flowing design was inspired by Persian 'flying' carpets. The design was photo-etched, then engraved before the dish was gently curved and enamelled with a myriad of transparent colours.
SARAH WILSON

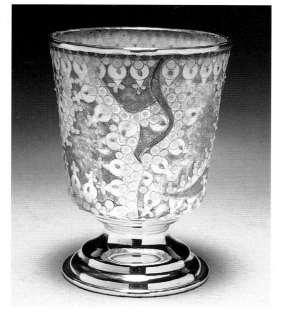

MATERIALS

OST OF THE MATERIALS USED IN ENAMELLING ARE OF A SPECIALIST NATURE, BUT THEY CAN BE OBTAINED FROM AN ENAMELLERS' SUPPLIER. BEGIN WITH THE SIMPLER PROJECTS AND BUILD UP YOUR COLLECTION OF MATERIALS AS YOU GAIN CONFIDENCE.

Acids and pickles Dilute solutions of sulphuric acid, alum and other acids are used to de-grease and de-oxidize metal before or after firing. Nitric acid, in various solutions, is used as an etchant and for the removal of oxidization.

Brush cleaner Use as a solvent for stopping-out varnish and for cleaning paintbrushes.

Ceramic fibre This can be moulded to support awkwardly shaped enamel work in the kiln during firing.

Copper and silver sheet/wire Available in various thicknesses and sections, which may be raised or drawn down as required. Copper, fine silver and fine gold wire are available in rectangular section, pre-annealed for *cloisonné*. For all enamelling, silver should be a minimum of .925 (Sterling) quality, and copper containing beryllium (used for electronics) should not be used.

Enamels Jewellery enamels are available in lump or powder form, with or without lead. Use transparent, opalescent or opaque enamels to create various effects. Painting enamels are either underglaze or onglaze, available in powder form. Flux enamels are clear, sometimes with added colour, producing an effect similar to clear or coloured varnish. Onglaze enamels are also available in tubes ready-mixed in a water- or oil- based medium. Lead-free jewellery enamels are also manufactured in liquid form for dip and spray applications. Enamels containing lead oxide are no longer available in the USA and are prohibited in many educational establishments. Leaded and lead-free enamels are incompatible as they have different firing and acid-resistant characteristics.

Enamel gum solution Several organic gum solutions are available, some in spray form. You can also use wallpaper paste, provided it does not contain fungicide. Dilute solution is used to hold *cloisonné* wires before firing, and a very weak solution is used to 'fix' powder enamel on to a curved surface or for stencilling. Use sparingly.

Epoxy resin glue Use this strong adhesive for the cold attachment of components and fittings, where hard soldering is inappropriate.

Etchants Solutions of acid can be used to etch designs in copper and silver.

Kaolin (ballclay, batwash) This can be used to prevent enamel adhesion to the firing support of the kiln floor.

Matting salts These give a frosted finish to enamel.

Mediums and thinners Prepared solutions are based in pine oil. However, pure aromatic oils such as oil of lavender, rosemary or cloves can also be used and are available from chemists (drugstores).

Mica This is used as a base for *plique-à-jour* enamelling of flat items.

PnP blue acetate film This is used to produce a photographic resist for acid etching.

Pumice powder Mixed with water to a slurry (paste), this is used to polish both enamel and metal. It is available from specialist suppliers and chemists (drugstores).

Resists These are applied to protect metal while other areas are etched. They are available from jewellers' suppliers.

Silver and gold foil 23.5 ct fine gold foil and .995 ct fine silver foil are sold in various thicknesses. Gilders' gold leaf is usually too thin for enamelling.

Solder Hard, 4N, 'IT', grade silver solder should be used for all soldering prior to enamelling. Easy grade silver solder may be used with care after enamelling assembly.

Washing (baking) soda crystals A solution of washing (baking) soda is used to neutralize acids.

Washing-up liquid (liquid soap) Use in solution with water to de-grease metal.

Water In hard-water areas, use purified water or rainwater. Limescale and additives can impair the clarity of transparent enamels in particular.

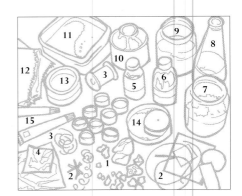

KEY

1 Enamels
2 Silver and copper wire, sheet and solder
3 Silver *cloisonné* wire
4 Gold and silver foil
5 Medium
6 Enamel gum solution
7 Washing (baking) soda crystals

8 Water
9 Matting salts
10 Resist
11 Washing-up liquid (liquid soap)
12 Cotton cloths
13 Brush cleaner
14 Pumice powder (with felt mop)
15 Epoxy resin glue

EQUIPMENT

THE MAIN PIECE OF EQUIPMENT THAT YOU WILL NEED FOR ENAMELLING IS A DOMESTIC-SIZED GAS OR ELECTRIC KILN. SPECIALIST EQUIPMENT IS AVAILABLE FROM ENAMELLERS' AND JEWELLERS' SUPPLIERS. A GOOD TOOL MERCHANT WILL BE ABLE TO SUPPLY ANY OTHER EQUIPMENT.

Brass brush Use a suede or other brass brush to clean metal after pickling. Do not use to clean stoned enamel as the brass may contaminate it.

Burnisher Use to raise a fine edge around a piece of metal and to polish out blemishes. You can use a tapestry needle stuck into a cork instead.

Carborundum stone Used with water, this is the traditional abrasive for enamel. Medium-grade is the most useful.

Containers Drop and spray bottles and strong-lidded plastic boxes are needed for enamels and other substances.

Craft knives and scalpels Use for various purposes such as cutting stencils.

Dental probes These and other stainless steel tools such as (forged) skewers can be used for the wet application of enamel.

Diamond-impregnated paper Available in sheet form with a self-adhesive backing, this is a cleaner and faster abrasive than carborundum, and it is invaluable for concave surfaces.

Doming block, swage block, mandrel and punches Available in steel, brass or hardwood, and used metal shape. Use with a hammer for steel and brass, and a mallet for hardwood.

Drill and drill bits Jewellers traditionally use a bow or Archimedes drill, but hand or electric pendant drills are fine.

Emery sticks (boards) Use to remove any marks left after filing. Alternatively, use offcuts (scraps) of dowel covered in emery paper (sandpaper).

Felt polishing mop Available in various sizes, this is impregnated with pumice powder and water to polish fired enamel. A felt polishing mop can be used with an electric polishing motor running at 900–1200 rpm.

Files Use hand files to remove burrs after cutting metal, and needle files to reach awkward places. Diamond files are used with water to abrade fired enamel.

Firing fork This is used to handle enamelled work, on a firing support, both in and out of the kiln. For jewellery and other lightweight work, you can use a large palette knife (spatula).

Firing support Use ready-made supports or make them from stainless steel sheet and mesh offcuts (scraps). Aluminium, bronze and titanium supports do not produce firescale with repeated use.

Glass fibre brush Use to clean enamel as it will not scratch metal and can reach awkward areas. Avoid direct contact with your hands as it can cause skin irritation.

Gravers Available in different shapes to carve cells from sheet metal.

Hammer A general-purpose medium-weight hammer is used for shaping, forming and riveting metal.

Kiln Electric kilns are insulated with fire-brick and take longer to heat up to firing temperature than gas-fired kilns, which are insulated with ceramic fibre. They are, however, comparatively inexpensive.

Linen or cotton fabric Clean, lint-free cloth such as sheeting (sheets) or handkerchiefs is used to remove excess water.

Mallet Use with wooden punches to shape metal without marking the surface.

Nail buffer Use to remove any marks from metal left after filing. Or use offcuts (scraps) of dowel covered in fine-grade emery paper (sandpaper).

Paintbrushes Use for stencilling and wet-applying enamel. Pure sable artists' brushes are traditional, but good-quality synthetic brushes cost less and will be unaffected by mediums and thinners.

Palettes Use to contain washed enamel ready for use, covered with purified water.

Pestle and mortar Use only vitrified porcelain to grind and wash enamels.

Piercing saw Use to cut shapes from sheet metal. The best saw blades are German or Swiss, Nos. 1–4/0.

Pliers Pliers are available in various profiles. Use to bend sheet metal or wire.

Pyrometer This temperature-measuring device is easily fitted to an electric kiln and is used for work such as annealing where exact temperature is critical.

Quills The butts of goose quills, cut to length, are used to wet-apply enamel without the risk of metal contamination. Available also from calligraphers' suppliers.

Regulator (thermostat) The supply to an electric kiln needs to be controlled to prevent the elements overheating. The alternative is to open the kiln door or switch off the supply at intervals.

Rolling mill Use to reduce the thickness of annealed sheet metal, to flatten wire and to impress patterns on metal.

Scriber, dividers, centre punch and rule Use to measure and mark out metal.

Sieves Use to apply dry enamel. Match the mesh size to the ground enamel.

Snips or shears Use to cut solder and thin wire to length. Sharp household scissors can also be used.

Soldering equipment As well as solder, you will need charcoal or heat-reflective soldering blocks and sheet, a gas blow-torch and borax-based flux (auflux).

Stiff bristle brush Use an old, clean nailbrush or toothbrush to apply pumice powder.

Tongs and tweezers To handle metal in and out of pickle or etchants use brass, copper or plastic tongs or tweezers. For fine work and *cloisonné* use fine stainless steel tweezers, also available from dental suppliers. For hot work use 20 cm (8 in) steel tweezers.

Wet-and-dry paper Useful for stoning enamel before the final firing and to give a matt finish.

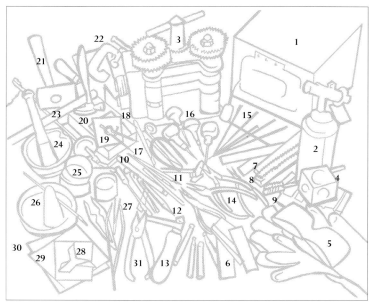

KEY

1 Kiln on heat resistant block
2 Blowtorch
3 Rolling mills
4 Doming block and punches, swage block
5 Safety goggles, rubber gloves, heat resistant gloves
6 Diamond-impregnated paper, carborundum stones
7 Wet-and-dry paper, emery sticks (boards)
8 Brass brush
9 Toothbrush
10 Glassbrush
11 Quills, stainless steel saunas, (forged) skewers, fine artist's paintbrush, dental probes
12 Scriber
13 Piercing saw
14 Pliers
15 Needle files
16 Gravers
17 Scissors, scalpel (craft knife)
18 Firing fork
19 Dividers
20 Soldering block
21 Hammer, mallet
22 Bench pin (peg) and clamp (G clamp)
23 Drill
24 Pestle and mortar
25 Sieves
26 Soldering flux (borax cone in dish, auflux)
27 Plastic, brass, stainless steel tweezers
28 Firing supports (trivet, mesh)
29 Mica
30 Ceramic fibre
31 Shears

BASIC TECHNIQUES

SOME TECHNIQUES, SUCH AS PREPARING METAL AND FIRING IN THE KILN, ARE COMMON TO ALL ENAMELLING PROJECTS. OTHERS, SUCH AS PHOTO-ETCHING, ARE USED IN SPECIFIC CASES. REFER BACK TO THESE GENERAL INSTRUCTIONS AS NECESSARY WHEN FOLLOWING THE STEPS IN THE PROJECTS.

HEALTH AND SAFETY

• Always work in a well-ventilated environment. If you are using chemicals, work near a sink.
• Never eat, drink or smoke.
• Store chemicals in labelled containers in a secure, dry place away from direct sunlight. Always read the manufacturer's instructions before use.
• Wear protective clothing (plastic goggles, face mask, strong rubber gloves and plastic apron) when using chemicals. Wear heat-resistant gloves and infra-red goggles when firing.
• Do not touch your eyes when using chemicals. Wash your hands after handling.
• Avoid breathing dust and fumes. Wear a dust mask when sifting dry enamels.
• Handle ceramic fibre and glass fibre products with care as they can cause skin or respiratory irritation.
• Keep an appropriate fire extinguisher and fire blanket ready for use.
• Have a first aid kit to hand, including neutralizing agents for the chemicals.
• When diluting concentrated acid with water, always add the acid to the water, *never* the reverse.
• Only dispose of small quantities of acid down the sink if your waste pipes are plastic, not lead. Flush with water.
• Stand the kiln and any work that is cooling after firing on a heat-protective surface such as ceramic tiles, marble or non-asbestos fireboard.
• Turn off the kiln when it is not needed for more than 30 minutes.

PREPARATION OF METAL (INCLUDING PICKLING)

Before enamelling, all metals must be de-greased and de-oxidized. De-oxidizing (also known as pickling) is done by placing the metal in a general pickle solution. A 10% solution of sulphuric acid, safety pickle or alum can be used as a general pickle.

1 To de-grease, abrade with emery paper (sandpaper), or with a slurry (paste) of pumice powder and a bristle brush. Copper may be treated in a general pickle; use a pair of tweezers to place in a general pickle solution. Do not use steel or nickel-plated tweezers to pickle copper and silver together – the silver will be plated with copper.

2 To remove oxidation completely from sterling or Britannia silver, cover the metal with neat nitric acid and swill the container gently until the metal appears white. Alternatively, heat silver with a blowtorch until it turns dull cherry red. Quench in cold water then place in 10% sulphuric acid solution until it turns white. Rinse and repeat three times.
 Fine silver does not oxidize and requires only brightening.

3 Brighten all metals with a brass brush and washing-up liquid (liquid soap) solution. Dry with a clean cotton cloth, without touching the area to be enamelled. Store under water for future use to prevent further oxidation.

ANNEALING

1 To make metal more malleable, anneal it by heating with a blowtorch to a cherry-red colour. Remove the flame, allow the metal to return to black then quench in cold water. Pickle the metal to remove the oxidation.

SOLDERING

It is best to design a piece so that the enamel section has as little soldering as possible. This will prevent enamel discolouration or bubbling. The parts to be soldered should fit neatly together. If necessary, support them with binding wire or tweezers so that they do not move during soldering.

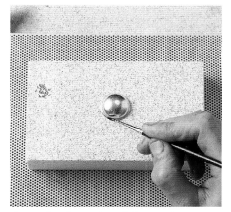

1 Apply a borax-based flux to the joint area.

2 Cut the solder into small pieces and apply them to the joint, using an old artist's paintbrush laden with flux (auflux).

3 Play a flame gently over the entire piece, drying the flux without letting it bubble. When the flux appears crystalline, intensify the flame on the joint area so that both parts of the joint heat up evenly until the solder melts.

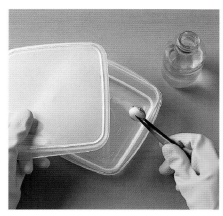

4 Cool the metal, then pickle it to remove fire stain and flux. Use the general pickle solution as described opposite or 5 ml (1 tsp) alum powder dissolved in 450 ml (¾ pint) warm water. Rinse the metal under running water, dry and remove any excess solder with a file.

METAL FORMING

1 To dome annealed metal, place it in an appropriately sized depression in a doming block and tap it into shape. Use a mallet with wooden punches and a hammer with steel punches. Shaping metal hardens it, so if a high dome is required you may need to anneal and clean the metal again before completing the shaping.

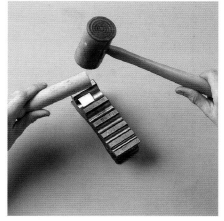

2 Metal can also be formed in a swage block, using the shaft of a doming punch. If the design is etched or roller printed, protect the surface from bruising with masking tape or thick paper.

ACID ETCHING

Always be careful when working with etchants. Wear heavy rubber gloves and safety goggles, and use only brass or plastic tweezers.

1 De-grease and de-oxidize the metal by pickling it then brighten with a brass brush and washing-up liquid (liquid soap) solution. Dry with a clean cotton cloth, taking care not to handle the metal with your fingers.

2 The back and edges of the piece need to be protected from the etchant. To do this paint on three thin coats of stopping-out varnish using on old artist's paintbrush. Ensure the back and edges are completely covered with stopping-out.

3 Leave to dry then paint the design on the front in varnish. The acid will etch away all the areas not covered by varnish so ensure the edges and corners are well protected.

4 Correct any mistakes and redefine the details of the design using a fine steel point.

5 Alternatively, fine designs can be created in reverse. Paint the entire surface with varnish then remove the areas to be etched with a fine steel point.

6 Wearing protective clothing, place the metal in an open plastic or glass container with 1 part neat nitric acid: 3 parts cold water. Gently stroke away bubbles, using a small feather. The length of time required to etch different metals varies considerably according to the etchant's age and temperature. For enamelling, the depth of etching should not exceed one-third of the thickness of the metal.

7 When the required depth is achieved, remove the metal with brass or plastic tweezers. Rinse under running water, using a glass fibre brush. Remove any remaining varnish with brush cleaner. Brighten the surface with a brass brush and washing-up liquid (liquid soap) solution.

PHOTO-ETCHING

Photo-etching is another method of producing enamelled designs. Instead of painting the design to be etched directly onto the metal surface, you produce a resist using PnP blue acetate film. Draw a high-contrast black-and-white design twice the size of the finished piece, ensuring that all lines are a minimum of 0.7 mm thick. The black will represent metal, and the white will represent the enamelled area in the piece you are creating. Reduce the design down to the actual size on a photocopier.

Photocopy this image, at high contrast, on to a sheet of PnP blue acetate film (emulsion-side up) to produce a photographic resist. Iron the resist on to the prepared metal (use a cotton/dry iron setting) until the image is fixed.

Paint the back and edges of the metal with stopping out varnish and place in a nitric acid solution as described in steps 6 and 7 opposite.

PREPARATION OF ENAMEL

Use a pestle and mortar to grind lump enamel. Ready-ground enamel is also available. Small, intricate designs and curved surfaces usually require more finely ground enamel than large, flat pieces.

1 Break up nuggets of enamel by wrapping them in a strong bag or clean cotton cloth and hitting them with a hammer. Rinse the pestle and mortar and place on a cork mat or folded dish towel to stop it slipping. Cover a small piece of enamel with filtered or purified water and, wearing protective goggles, hit it with the pestle until it resembles granulated sugar. Repeat with another piece until you have enough enamel for the project.

2 If necessary, add more water to keep the enamel covered. Holding the pestle upright, firmly grind the enamel with a circular action. The grinding time varies – the enamel is ready when it feels soft and powdery.

3 Allow the enamel to settle for a few seconds, then carefully pour off the water. Rinse the enamel with clean water until the water runs clear and the ground enamel is uniform in colour.

4 For wet application, pour the enamel into a ceramic or glass palette and cover with water and another palette or lid. For dry application, or sifting, pour off as much water as possible. Spread the remaining paste on to cooking foil, cover and dry on top of the kiln or a radiator.

DRY APPLICATION OF ENAMEL

1 De-grease the metal by scrubbing it thoroughly with a brass brush and washing-up liquid (liquid soap) solution. Dry it with a clean cotton cloth, without touching the area to be enamelled.

2 Cover the area to be enamelled with enamel gum, applying it thinly.

3 Place the metal on a piece of paper. Select a sieve the same mesh size as the enamel powder, hold it 6 cm (2½ in) above the metal and tap gently.

4 Carefully lift the metal and clean any excess enamel powder from the sides with an artist's paintbrush. Place the metal on a trivet, and ensure that it is not knocked or moved before firing.

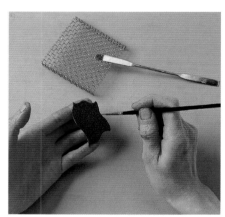

5 On following layers, if you wish, you can paint a design in the enamel gum before sifting the enamel, or use a stencil. Alternatively, you can scratch a design in the applied enamel with a metal point or an artist's paintbrush before firing.

WET APPLICATION OF ENAMEL

Wet enamel should be applied with a fine artist's paintbrush, quill or stainless steel point fashioned from a (forged) skewer. Unused prepared enamels can be stored covered with purified water, although they will deteriorate with prolonged storage. Enamel should be applied in several thin layers rather than one thick layer.

1 Pour off excess water from the prepared enamel and tip the container so that the waterline is halfway up the enamel. Take the enamel from just above the waterline. Apply it evenly and thinly, so that no metal is showing. Ensure it is pushed well into any corners, as it will draw back slightly during firing.

2 Hold a clean cotton cloth to the edge of the enamel and draw off any excess water. Do not touch the enamel or it will impair the finish of the fired enamel. Fire the piece as soon as possible.

KILN FIRING

The firing temperature of the kiln should be between 900°C/1652°F for small items and a maximum of 1000°C/1832°F for large pieces. Kiln firing times vary according to the thickness of the metal, the kiln temperature and the fact that enamels fuse at slightly different temperatures. Using heat-protective gloves and goggles, place the enamel near the kiln to remove any moisture, which is indicated when no more steam rises from it and the enamel surface appears more crystalline. When placing the object in the kiln, check that the trivet or other firing support holds the piece securely without wobbling, and that the enamel doesn't touch it. If you do not need the kiln for more than 30 minutes, lower the temperature or turn it off.

1 When first placed in the kiln, the enamel colour will lighten. The metal will change colour and oxidize as it is heated. Later, the enamel colour will darken but it will still appear matt and granular.

2 The enamel will then start to melt and to look uneven but shiny.

3 When fully fired, the enamel will look smooth and shiny. If it pulls away from the edges and discolours, it is overfired.

It is best to slightly underfire the first layers of enamel until they are shiny but still rippled, and keep the highest firing for the last. If you are firing a large piece, turn it round in the kiln halfway through to ensure even firing.

FINISHING

1 For a smooth finish, abrade the enamel with carborundum stones, diamond files, diamond-impregnated paper or wet-and-dry paper, all available in different grades. Use plenty of water and work all over the surface, constantly changing direction. The enamel will appear matt, making evident any low spots that may need to be filled and re-fired. Remove the abrasive residue by scrubbing the whole piece with a glass fibre brush or toothbrush and water. Dry with a clean cotton cloth – do not touch the enamel surface.

2 Re-fire the piece. When cool, place in a cold 10% pickle solution. Some enamel colours should be protected with a resist such as nail polish. Polish the enamel and metal with a slurry (paste) of 240-mesh pumice powder and water, using a felt polishing mop either by hand or using a motor running at 900–1200 rpm. This may be followed by rouge polishing. Do not use tripoli as it abrades enamel.

FLEUR-DE-LIS BOOKMARK

THIS STUNNING HERALDIC DESIGN IS VERY SIMPLE TO ACHIEVE, USING A SILVER FOIL MOTIF AGAINST A RICH BLUE ENAMEL BACKGROUND. EXPERIMENT WITH OTHER MOTIFS AND COLOURS. THREADED WITH A LENGTH OF RIBBON, THE PLAQUE BECOMES A DISTINCTIVE BOOKMARK.

1 Trace the template at the back of the book. Using metal snips, cut out the bookmark shape from the copper sheet. Drill a large hole in one corner for the ribbon. File the edges smooth.

2 Support the copper on a small bottle top or similar item. Grind and clean the enamel. Sift over an even layer of dry enamel, using a small sieve. The enamel should not fill the bookmark's hole. Transfer to a trivet with a palette knife (spatula) and fire in the kiln.

3 Clean the firescale from the back with emery paper (sandpaper). Sift some dry enamel as before over the back of the copper and fire again.

4 Trace the fleur-de-lis motif on to tracing paper. Sandwich the silver foil in the tracing paper and cut out carefully. Alternatively, use a readymade paper punch with a suitable motif to cut out the foil.

5 Gently lift the foil with a damp paintbrush and set it on the copper, feeding a little water underneath to position it. Use a little enamel gum if necessary. Blot away any excess water and place the piece gently in the kiln. Fire until the foil barely sinks into the enamel.

6 Sift another layer of enamel over the surface and fire again. Leave to cool, then clean the edges and thread with ribbon to complete the bookmark.

MATERIALS AND EQUIPMENT YOU WILL NEED

TRACING PAPER AND PENCIL • METAL SNIPS • 0.5 MM THICK COPPER SHEET • DRILL • FILE • BOTTLE TOP • PESTLE AND MORTAR • TRANSPARENT ROYAL BLUE ENAMEL • SMALL SIEVE • TRIVET • PALETTE KNIFE (SPATULA) • KILN AND FIRING EQUIPMENT • EMERY PAPER (SANDPAPER) • SILVER FOIL • SMALL, SHARP SCISSORS • PAPER PUNCH WITH SUITABLE MOTIF (OPTIONAL) • FINE ARTIST'S PAINTBRUSH • ENAMEL GUM (OPTIONAL) • CLEAN COTTON CLOTH • RIBBON

DOOR PLAQUE

MAKE A PERSONALIZED ENAMEL SIGN TO DISPLAY YOUR HOUSE NUMBER OR BUSINESS LOGO, USING A SIMPLE STENCIL TECHNIQUE. THIS BLUE- AND-WHITE DESIGN IS PRACTICAL AND EYE-CATCHING, BUT ALSO HAS A LOVELY TRADITIONAL LOOK.

1 Trace the template at the back of the book and transfer on to the copper. Drill two holes as indicated to fit the size of your screws. Cut out the shape with a piercing saw, then clean with a glass fibre brush and pumice powder under running water. Rinse very thoroughly.

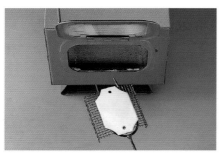

2 Grind and clean the enamels. Place the plaque on a trivet and sift over an even layer of white enamel. Fire in the kiln. Let cool then clean the oxidation off the back with emery paper (sandpaper).

3 Trace numbers or motifs on to ordinary paper, enlarging them on a photocopier if necessary to fit the plaque. Cut around each shape carefully with a craft knife (scalpel) to make stencils.

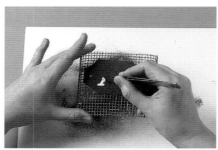

4 Spray a thin layer of enamel gum on to the plaque. Position the stencils then sift on a even layer of blue enamel. Using tweezers, carefully lift off the stencils.

5 If any grains of blue enamel appear on the white, remove them with a fine paintbrush.

6 Fire the plaque. Leave to cool, then remove the oxidation from the back. Attach the plaque using the brass screws.

MATERIALS AND EQUIPMENT YOU WILL NEED

TRACING PAPER AND PENCIL • 1 MM THICK COPPER SHEET • DRILL • PIERCING SAW • GLASS FIBRE BRUSH • PUMICE POWDER • PESTLE AND MORTAR • OPAQUE ENAMELS: WHITE AND ROYAL BLUE • TRIVET • SIEVE • KILN AND FIRING EQUIPMENT • EMERY PAPER (SANDPAPER) • PAPER • PHOTOCOPIER (OPTIONAL) • CRAFT KNIFE (SCALPEL) • RULER • DILUTE GUM SOLUTION IN AN ATOMIZER • TWEEZERS • FINE ARTIST'S PAINTBRUSH • SCREWDRIVER • 2 BRASS SCREWS

GEOMETRIC POTSTAND

ONE SIMPLE STENCIL DESIGN IS REPEATED FOUR TIMES, USING A DIFFERENT COLOUR FOR EACH BASE LAYER BEFORE THE ENAMELLED PANELS ARE ARRANGED TOGETHER ON A STAINED WOODEN BASE. FIRING DIRECTLY ON TO COPPER PRODUCES SUBTLE VARIATIONS OF WARM AND COOL COPPER TONES.

1 To make the stencil, draw a 5 cm (2 in) square on thin card (cardboard). Draw an irregular striped design and cut out.

3 Remove firescale with emery paper (sandpaper). Rinse and dry. Apply kaolin (ball clay, bat wash) over the counter enamel. Allow to dry.

5 Place the stencil on top of each square. Sift over the deep blue enamel and fire. When cool, clean with a slurry of pumice powder and a toothbrush. Repeat for a stronger colour.

2 Clean the copper squares. Because the squares are relatively large, you will need to apply counter enamel to the back of the pieces to keep them flat. Use a sieve to apply dry counter enamel to the back of each square. Fire in the kiln and let cool.

4 Cover a 1 cm (½ in) strip at the top of each square with card (cardboard). Sieve over one of the fluxes. Remove the card, then brush away any stray grains of enamel. Fire and clean as before.

6 Arrange the copper squares on the MDF (medium-density fiberboard) base, leaving an even border around the edge, and glue.

MATERIALS AND EQUIPMENT YOU WILL NEED

PENCIL AND RULER • THIN CARD (CARDBOARD) • CRAFT KNIFE OR SMALL, SHARP SCISSORS • 4 PIECES OF 0.8 MM THICK COPPER SQUARES, 5 CM (2 IN) SQUARE • 100-MESH SIEVE • COUNTER ENAMEL • KILN AND FIRING EQUIPMENT • EMERY PAPER (FINE SANDPAPER) • KAOLIN (BALL CLAY, BATWASH) • BRUSH FOR KAOLIN (BALL CLAY, BAT WASH) • THICK CARD (CARDBOARD) • BLUE, HARD SILVER, HARD COPPER AND NORMAL FLUX • SMALL DECORATOR'S PAINTBRUSH • TRANSPARENT DEEP BLUE ENAMEL • PUMICE POWDER • TOOTHBRUSH • 12 CM (4½ IN) SQUARE OF MDF (MEDIUM-DENSITY FIBERBOARD), STAINED BLACK OR DARK BLUE • EPOXY RESIN GLUE

STARGAZER EARRINGS

THE DESIGN FOR THESE JOLLY EARRINGS IS TRANSFERED TO A PAIR OF SILVER BLANKS USING THE PHOTO-ETCHING TECHNIQUE. WHEN USING A DESIGN LIKE THIS, REMEMBER THAT IT SHOULD BE APPLIED TO THE SECOND EARRING IN REVERSE SO THAT THE FINISHED PIECES ARE SYMMETRICAL.

1 Photocopy the template at the back of the book to produce a high contrast black-and-white design. The design needs to be photo-etched on to the earring blanks or silver sheet. The design should be twice the size of the finished piece for quantity commercial photo-etching or actual size for use with PnP blue acetate film. Cut out the shapes with a piercing saw, place each earring in a clamp and file the edges straight.

2 Polish the edges of the earrings with a fine emery (sand) stick to remove any scratch marks left after filing.

3 Secure each earring in turn on your work surface with masking tape. Centre punch and drill a hole.

4 Place each earring into the doming block. Tap with a doming punch and mallet to create the desired domed shape. ▶

MATERIALS AND EQUIPMENT YOU WILL NEED

SILVER EARRING BLANKS, TO FIT THE TEMPLATE, OR 1.1 MM THICK SILVER SHEET •
PnP BLUE ACETATE FILM • PIERCING SAW • RING CLAMP • FILE • FINE EMERY (SAND) STICK • MASKING TAPE • CENTRE PUNCH • DRILL •
WOODEN DOMING BLOCK • WOODEN DOMING PUNCH • MALLET • NITRIC ACID • BRASS BRUSH • WASHING-UP LIQUID (LIQUID SOAP) SOLUTION •
PESTLE AND MORTAR • TRANSPARENT ENAMELS • CONTAINERS FOR ENAMELS • ENAMEL GUM • FINE ARTIST'S PAINTBRUSH OR QUILL •
KILN AND FIRING EQUIPMENT • DIAMOND-IMPREGNATED PAPER • FINE-GRADE EMERY PAPER (FINE SANDPAPER) • PICKLE SOLUTION •
PUMICE POWDER OR FELT POLISHING MOP (OPTIONAL) • EARRING WIRES • FINE JEWELLERY PLIERS

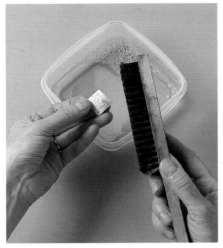

5 De-oxidize the earrings by placing them in nitric acid for a few minutes, then rinsing in cold water. Using a brass brush, brush with washing-up liquid (liquid soap) solution until shiny. Hold by the edges.

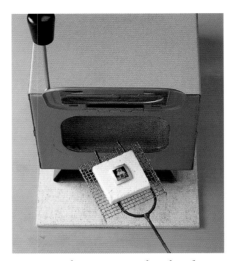

7 Leave the earrings to dry, then fire in the kiln until the enamel is molten. Leave to cool. Apply further layers of enamel and fire each time until the *champlevé* cells are full.

9 Leave to cool. Abrade the back of the earrings with emery paper (fine sandpaper), then place in pickle solution to remove oxidation.

6 Grind and clean the enamels, then add a drop of enamel gum. Apply the wet enamels, using a paintbrush or quill. Take care not to mix the colours.

8 Using medium-grade diamond-impregnated paper and water, abrade the enamel until you expose the silver design. Apply more enamel to any shiny areas, then repeat the firing and abrading and rinsing. Refire to glaze the surface.

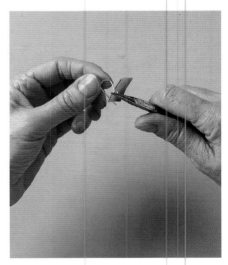

10 Polish both sides of the earrings if desired. Carefully open the ear wires with the jewellery pliers and insert through the drilled holes. Squeeze the wires gently together to close.

NAPKIN RINGS

HERE A LENGTH OF COPPER PIPE HAS BEEN TRANSFORMED INTO A RICHLY DECORATED SET OF NAPKIN RINGS. THE PATTERN IS SCRATCHED INTO THE BASE LAYER OF ENAMEL USING THE SGRAFFITO TECHNIQUE BEFORE DECORATING WITH ONGLAZE COLOURS.

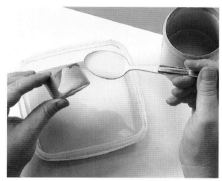

2 Coat the outer surface of each ring with liquid flux using a spoon. Leave to dry before coating the insides.

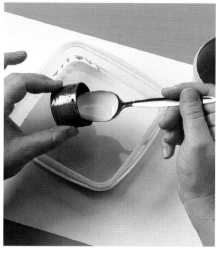

4 Coat the rings with liquid white enamel and leave to dry. Pierce the holes again as necessary.

1 Using a hacksaw, cut the pipe into 2.5 cm (1 in) wide rings. Drill holes about 2 cm (¾ in) apart along one edge of each ring and file the edges. Anneal and clean the metal. Cut or purchase small copper discs 2.25 cm (⅞ in), as many discs as there are holes in the rings. Drill a hole near the edge of each disc.

3 Pierce the holes with a sharp point to remove dried flux. Fire the rings – the thick walls of the pipe will take a lot of heat out of the kiln so increase the firing temperature to compensate.

MATERIALS AND EQUIPMENT YOU WILL NEED

HACKSAW • 4 CM (1½ IN) DIAMETER COPPER PIPE • FILE • DRILL • COPPER DISCS, 2.25CM (⅞ IN) • PENCIL AND PAPER • LIQUID ENAMEL FLUX • METAL SPOON • TOOL WITH SHARP POINT • KILN AND FIRING EQUIPMENT • LIQUID WHITE ENAMEL • SEWING NEEDLE • CORK • SOFT NATURAL-FIBRE BRUSH • ONGLAZE CERAMIC COLOURS: YELLOW AND RED • PALETTE • FINE ARTIST'S PAINTBRUSH • PAPERCLIPS • SMALL TRIVET • FINE-GRADE WET-AND-DRY PAPER • JUMP RINGS • SMALL PLIERS

5 Using a sharp point, mark notches at the top and bottom of the ring. Draw straight diagonal lines from the bottom notches to the top notches to create a diamond pattern. Add fine details using a needle stuck in a cork. Gently brush off the dried enamel powder (never blow it). Fire the ring.

6 Mix the onglaze colours on a palette. Paint a diamond pattern using a fine paintbrush as shown. Leave to dry, then fire following the manufacturer's instructions.

7 Bend a paperclip and use it to suspend a small copper disc while you coat it with liquid white enamel. Leave to dry on the paperclip. Remove from the paperclip and fire on a small trivet that supports the edges.

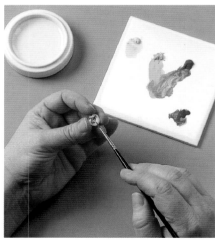

8 Paint the discs with the onglaze colours and then fire.

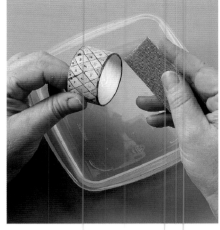

9 Clean the edges of the ring and copper discs with wet-and-dry paper and water.

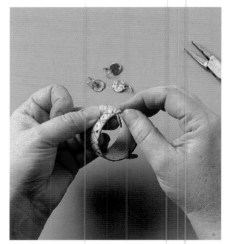

10 Using jump rings and pliers, attach the discs around the top of each ring through the drilled holes.

BIRD PIN

THIS STYLIZED — AND STYLISH — BIRD, CARRYING A HEART IN HIS BEAK, IS ENAMELLED ON SILVER TO MAKE AN ATTRACTIVE LAPEL PIN. CUT OUT THIS SIMPLE SHAPE FOLLOWING THE TEMPLATE AT THE BACK OF THE BOOK. IN THIS PROJECT, THE OPAQUE ENAMEL COLOURS CREATE A MATT SURFACE.

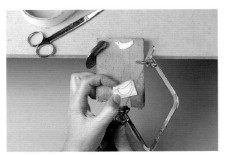

1 Trace the template at the back of the book. Stick the tracing on to the silver sheet using double-sided tape and cut out with a piercing saw. Drill a hole so that you can thread the saw blade through to reach the area between the heart and the bird.

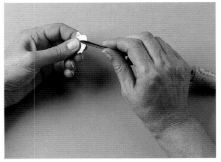

3 Burnish the edges of the bird to provide a 'grip' for the enamel to adhere to. Grind and clean the enamels then add a drop of enamel gum and water to cover.

5 Place the bird on top of the kiln to dry, then fire it. Apply two more layers of enamel, firing each layer.

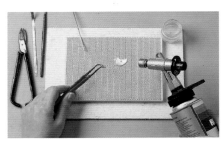

2 Cut and file a piece of silver tube 5 mm (¼ in) long. Solder it in an upright position on to the back, using hard solder. For the pin, cut a 6 cm (2⅖ in) length of the silver wire. Bend with pliers 0.5 mm in from one end to make a right angle.

4 De-grease the silver using a glass fibre brush and water. Place the bird on a trivet and apply the enamel using a paintbrush or quill.

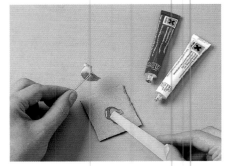

6 Abrade the enamel with diamond-impregnated paper and water. Smooth with the wet-and-dry paper and water. Rinse. Leave the enamel surface matt. Buff the plain silver side of the bird until it shines. Glue the pin into the tube.

MATERIALS AND EQUIPMENT YOU WILL NEED

TRACING PAPER AND PENCIL • DOUBLE-SIDED TAPE • 1.2 MM THICK SILVER SHEET • PIERCING SAW • DRILL • SILVER TUBE AND CORRESPONDING WIRE FOR THE PIN (INNER DIAMETER OF TUBE TO MATCH THICKNESS OF WIRE) • SOLDERING EQUIPMENT • HARD SOLDER • PLIERS • BURNISHER • PESTLE AND MORTAR • OPAQUE ENAMELS: WHITE, BRIGHT RED AND MID-BLUE • BLACK TRANSPARENT ENAMEL • CONTAINERS FOR ENAMELS • ENAMEL GUM • GLASS FIBRE BRUSH • TRIVET • FINE ARTIST'S PAINTBRUSH OR QUILL • KILN AND FIRING EQUIPMENT • DIAMOND-IMPREGNATED PAPER • FINE-GRADE WET-AND-DRY PAPER • NAIL BUFFER • EPOXY RESIN GLUE

STRIPED NECKLACE

WET-APPLYING ENAMEL ON TO BEADS AND OTHER ROUND OBJECTS IS EASIER IF IT IS GROUND VERY FINELY AND YOU CONTROL THE AMOUNT OF WATER CAREFULLY. FOR A FROSTED FINISH, PLACE THE ENAMELLED BEADS IN MATTING SALTS FOR 2–3 MINUTES BEFORE PICKLING.

1 Using dividers, mark unequal stripes at random along the silver tubing.

2 Using a needle file, carefully make straight-sided grooves around the circumference of the tubing to a depth of 0.3 mm. Try to keep them as even in depth as possible. Alternatively, turn the grooves on a lathe.

3 Using a piercing saw, cut off unequal lengths of tubing between the recesses to make the beads. ▶

MATERIALS AND EQUIPMENT YOU WILL NEED

DIVIDERS • 50 CM (20 IN) OF 4 MM (³⁄₁₆ IN) DIAMETER THICK-WALLED, SILVER JOINT TUBING • SQUARE OR TRIANGULAR NEEDLE FILE • LATHE (OPTIONAL) • PIERCING SAW WITH FINE BLADE • TUBE CUTTER OR PIN VICE • FILE • WET-AND-DRY PAPER • BALL FRAIZE • COPPER OR SILVER WIRE • BRASS BRUSH • WASHING-UP LIQUID (LIQUID SOAP) SOLUTION • PESTLE AND MORTAR • TRANSPARENT ENAMELS OF YOUR CHOICE • CONTAINERS FOR ENAMELS • STAINLESS STEEL WIRE • FINE ARTIST'S PAINTBRUSH OR QUILL • CLEAN COTTON CLOTH • KILN AND FIRING EQUIPMENT • DIAMOND FILE OR CARBORUNDUM STONE • PICKLE SOLUTION • THREAD AND CLASP FOR STRINGING NECKLACE OR FINE SILVER CHAIN • CO-ORDINATING BEADS (OPTIONAL)

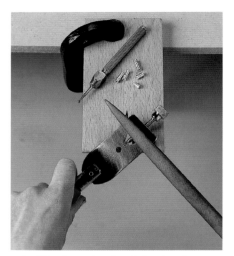

4 File the ends of each bead and smooth with wet-and-dry paper. Counter sink the central hole using a ball fraize.

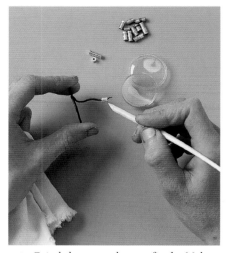

6 Grind the enamels very finely. Make several stainless steel wire spirals to hold each bead firmly, as shown. Wet-apply the enamel, using a fine artist's paintbrush or quill. Draw off excess water with a clean cloth before firing.

8 Thread each bead on a cranked length of stainless steel. Abrade each bead and smooth with wet-and-dry paper, rotating the wired bead. Temporarily thread several beads on to a length of copper or silver wire. Rinse before and after pickling.

5 Temporarily thread several beads on to a loop of wire and scrub with a brass brush and washing-up liquid (liquid soap) solution.

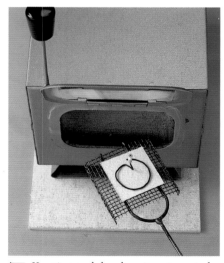

7 Keeping each bead on its wire spiral, fire in the kiln and leave to cool, still on the wire. Apply further layers of the same colour until each recess is full. Fire between each layer of enamel.

9 String the enamelled beads, perhaps interspersing them with co-ordinating beads. Alternatively, thread them on their own on to a fine silver chain and add a clasp.

NIGHT AND DAY CLOCK FACE

USE DRY ENAMEL TO COVER A COPPER CIRCLE WITH COMPLEMENTARY COLOURS, WHICH BLEND TOGETHER IN THE KILN. THE HOURS ARE MARKED WITH ELEGANT TWISTED COPPER WIRE NUMERALS AND GLASS BEADS FUSED INTO THE ENAMEL FACE.

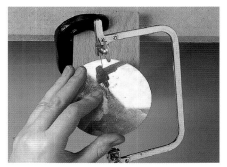

1 Drill a hole through the centre of the copper circle. Slip the saw blade through the hole, tighten the saw frame and cut out a small circle with a radius of 4 mm (³⁄₁₆ in) to fit the spindle.

2 Clean the copper under running water using pumice powder and a glass fibre brush. Rinse thoroughly and leave to dry.

3 Paint one side of the copper with enamel gum and stand on a trivet. Using a sieve, sift over an even layer of both enamels, one colour on each half. Blend the colours together in the centre.

4 Fire in the kiln until the enamel texture is like orange peel. Leave to cool.

5 Clean the back of the copper with a brass brush and washing-up liquid (liquid soap) solution. Dry with a clean, soft cloth.

6 Using pliers, cut lengths of wire and bend them to make the numerals, following the templates at the back of the book. Clean with a glass fibre brush and washing-up liquid (liquid soap) solution. ▶

MATERIALS AND EQUIPMENT YOU WILL NEED

DRILL • CIRCLE OF 1 MM THICK SHEET COPPER, 9 CM (3½ IN) DIAMETER, TO FIT TEMPLATE • PIERCING SAW • PUMICE POWDER • GLASS FIBRE BRUSH • ENAMEL GUM • SMALL DECORATOR'S PAINTBRUSH • TRIVET • SIEVE • OPAQUE ENAMELS: TURQUOISE AND BRIGHT BLUE • KILN AND FIRING EQUIPMENT • BRASS BRUSH • WASHING-UP LIQUID (LIQUID SOAP) SOLUTION • CLEAN COTTON CLOTH • HALF-ROUND AND ROUND-NOSED PLIERS • 1 MM THICK COPPER WIRE • WIRE (STEEL) WOOL • TWEEZERS • 8 SMALL ORANGE-COLOURED GLASS BEADS • 0.8 MM THICK COPPER WIRE (OPTIONAL) • BATTERY-OPERATED CLOCK MECHANISM WITH HANDS • SCREWDRIVER

7 Dip the numerals in enamel gum and position on the clock face. Let dry. Fire until the numerals have partially sunk into the enamel. Leave to cool then remove the oxidation from the back using wire (steel) wool.

9 Fire again until the beads have partially melted into the enamel. Leave to cool. Clean the numerals with pumice powder and washing-up liquid (liquid soap) solution, using a glass fibre brush. Then remove the oxidation from the back of the clock, using wire (steel) wool.

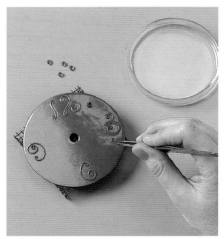

8 Using tweezers, dip the beads in enamel gum and position between the numerals as shown.

10 Cut and file the readymade clock hands to fit or make your own, using 0.8 mm copper wire and left-over copper sheet. Fit the clock mechanism through the hole and screw in place. Attach the hands.

MULTICOLOURED BUTTONS

MAKE A SET OF THESE WONDERFUL BUTTONS IN ANY SIZE, TO SUIT A SPECIAL GARMENT. THEY ARE DECORATED WITH A DELICATE SCATTERING OF TINY GOLD OR SILVER SHAPES AND DABS OF BRIGHTLY COLOURED ENAMEL, AND THEY ARE VERY QUICK AND EASY TO MAKE.

1 Drill two large holes side by side in the centre of each copper disc.

2 Clean the copper with pumice powder and water, using a toothbrush.

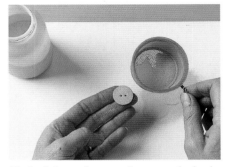

3 Lightly apply enamel gum to the back of each button. Using a sieve, apply enamel, using different colours. Leave to dry, then fire in the kiln. Clean the fronts and repeat, supporting the buttons on stilts. Apply a second layer of enamel if necessary.

4 Using scissors, cut tiny squares and triangles off the end of the gold or silver wire. Punch holes in the silver sheet to make tiny circles.

5 Decorate the buttons with the metal shapes, secured with enamel gum. Moisten a little enamel powder with enamel gum to make a paste, then apply in small dots with a fine paintbrush.

6 Support the buttons on stilts and fire in the kiln until the enamel dots have fused. When cool, remove oxidation by cleaning with pumice powder and water, using a toothbrush.

MATERIALS AND EQUIPMENT YOU WILL NEED

DRILL • 0.9 MM THICK COPPER DISCS, SIZE AS REQUIRED • PUMICE POWDER • TOOTHBRUSH • ENAMEL GUM • BRUSH • SIEVE • OPAQUE ENAMELS IN VARIOUS COLOURS • KILN AND FIRING EQUIPMENT • STILTS TO FIT BUTTONS • SCISSORS • FLAT GOLD OR SILVER *CLOISONNÉ* WIRE • PAPER HOLE PUNCH • 0.15 MM SILVER SHEET • FINE ARTIST'S PAINTBRUSH

PET BROOCH

REPRODUCE THIS JAUNTY CHARACTER BY TRACING THE TEMPLATE AT THE BACK OF THE BOOK AND PHOTO-ETCHING THE DESIGN ON TO A SQUARE BROOCH, LEAVING A GENEROUS FRAME OF SILVER. FOLLOW THE ENAMEL COLOURS SHOWN HERE OR CHOOSE YOUR OWN.

1 Photocopy the template at the back of the book to produce a high contrast black and white design. The design needs to be photo-etched on to the brooch blank or silver sheet (see Basic Techniques section and Suppliers). The design should be twice the size of the finished piece for quantity commercial photo-etching or actual size for use with PnP blue acetate film. Cut out the brooch shape with a piercing saw, place it in a clamp and file the edges straight.

2 Polish the edges of the brooch with a fine emery stick (board) to remove any scratch marks left by the file.

3 Place the annealed brooch blank into the doming block. Tap lightly with the punch and mallet until it is slightly domed.

4 De-oxidize the earrings by placing in nitric acid for a few minutes then rinsing in cold water. Using a brass brush, brush with water and washing-up liquid (liquid soap) until shiny. Hold by the edges only. ▶

MATERIALS AND EQUIPMENT YOU WILL NEED

TRACING PAPER AND BLACK PEN • SILVER BROOCH BLANK, TO FIT THE TEMPLATE OR SILVER SHEET • PnP BLUE ACETATE FILM (IF USED) • PIERCING SAW • RING CLAMP • FILE • FINE EMERY STICK • WOODEN DOMING BLOCK • WOODEN DOMING PUNCH • MALLET • NITRIC ACID • BRASS BRUSH • WASHING-UP LIQUID (LIQUID SOAP) • PESTLE AND MORTAR • TRANSPARENT ENAMELS • CONTAINERS FOR ENAMELS • ENAMEL GUM • FINE ARTIST'S PAINTBRUSH OR QUILL • KILN AND FIRING EQUIPMENT • DIAMOND-IMPREGNATED PAPER • EMERY PAPER (FINE SANDPAPER) • TRIVET • SOLDERING EQUIPMENT • BROOCH CATCH AND JOINT • EASY SOLDER • PICKLE SOLUTION (SEE BASIC TECHNIQUES) • TOOTHBRUSH • PUMICE POWDER • PARALLEL PLIERS

5 Grind and clean the enamels, then add a drop of enamel gum. Apply the wet enamels, using a paintbrush or quill. Leave to dry on top of the kiln.

6 Fire in the kiln until the enamel is molten. Leave to cool. Apply further layers of enamel, firing in between each layer, until the cells appear full.

7 Using medium-grade diamond-impregnated paper and water, abrade the enamel until you expose the silver design and rinse. Apply more enamel to any shiny areas then repeat the firing and abrading. Polish with fine-grade diamond-impregnated paper, rinse, then refire to glaze the surface.

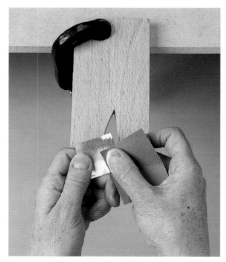

8 Leave to cool then remove the oxidation from the back of the brooch with emery paper (fine sandpaper).

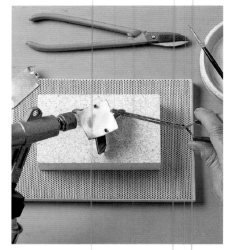

9 Place the brooch upside down on a trivet so that only the edges touch. Solder on the brooch catch and joint with easy solder. Leave to cool, then place in the pickle solution. Rinse, then clean using a toothbrush and a slurry of pumice powder.

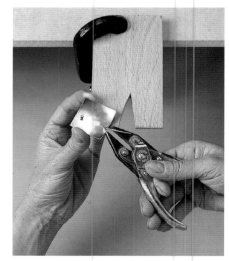

10 Polish the brooch if desired. Cut the brooch pin to length and place it in the ball joint. Using parallel pliers, squeeze carefully to rivet the pin in place.

SHIELD EARRINGS

THIS DELICATE TEXTURED SURFACE IS CREATED BY IMPRESSING THE SILVER WITH WATERCOLOUR PAPER THEN APPLYING TWO ENAMEL COLOURS AND FLUX TO CREATE A MARBLED EFFECT. SMALL JAGGED PIECES OF SILVER FOIL ARE FIRED BETWEEN THE ENAMEL LAYERS.

1 Cut a piece of watercolour paper slightly larger than the silver sheet. Anneal the silver and remove the oxidation. Place the silver sheet on top of the paper and run them together through the rolling mill, with the rollers tightly clamped down.

2 Trace the template at the back of the book, reversing it for the second earring. Attach the tracings to the silver with double-sided tape.

3 Using a piercing saw, cut out the shield shapes. File the edges. Drill a 1 mm hole in two of the same diagonally opposed corners of each shield. ▶

MATERIALS AND EQUIPMENT YOU WILL NEED

SCISSORS • SMALL PIECE OF ROUGH-TEXTURED WATERCOLOUR PAPER • 0.8MM THICK SILVER SHEET, TO FIT TWO EARRING TEMPLATES • ROLLING MILL • TRACING PAPER AND PENCIL • DOUBLE-SIDED TAPE • PIERCING SAW • FILE • DRILL • BURNISHER • BRASS BRUSH • WASHING-UP LIQUID (LIQUID SOAP) • CLEAN COTTON CLOTH • PESTLE AND MORTAR • TRANSPARENT ENAMELS: MAUVE AND PALE YELLOW-GREEN • CONTAINERS FOR ENAMELS • FINE ARTIST'S PAINTBRUSH OR QUILL • FLUX • KILN AND FIRING EQUIPMENT • TRIVET • CRAFT KNIFE • OFFCUTS (SCRAPS) OF FINE SILVER FOIL • COTTON CLOTH • DIAMOND FILE OR CARBORUNDUM STONE • WET-AND-DRY PAPER • EARRING WIRES • ROUND-NOSED PLIERS • 2 SMALL DOMED SILVER DISCS, FROSTED BEADS, AND BEAD PINS

4 Burnish around the sides to raise an edge to contain the enamel. Scrub the shields with a brass brush and washing-up liquid (liquid soap) solution, rinse and dry.

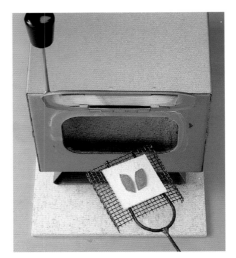

6 Fire the first layer in the kiln and leave to cool.

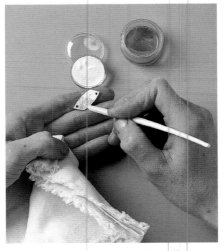

8 When cool, wet-apply the yellow-green enamel over the foil. Apply flux to all other areas and fire. Finally, fire a final layer using flux only.

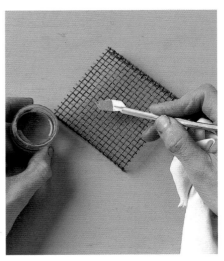

5 Grind and clean the enamels. Using a fine paintbrush or quill, wet-apply the flux and mauve enamel randomly to create a marbled effect. Ensure that they do not run into the drilled holes.

7 Using a craft knife, cut jagged pieces of silver foil. Moisten the fired enamel with water and apply the pieces of foil in a broken S-shaped line, using a damp paintbrush. Draw off excess water with a clean cotton cloth. Wet-apply a spot of flux to one corner of each shield and fire. When the flux has fused, the foil will have adhered to the enamel.

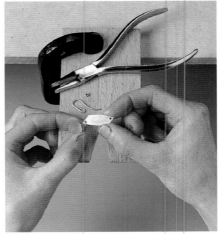

9 Abrade the fired surface using a diamond file, then rinse and fill in any low spots with more enamel and re-fire. Remove excess enamel from the edges then finish all sides of the shields with fine-grade wet-and-dry paper and rinse. Attach the earring wires. Add beads, bead pins and discs for decoration, if desired.

ABSTRACT ART KEYRING

THIS UNUSUAL DESIGN IS COMPOSED OF TINY PIECES OF COLOURED ENAMEL THREADS AND SILVER *CLOISONNÉ* WIRE LIGHTLY FUSED ON TO AN ENAMEL BASE. THE KEYRING, INCLUDING THE HOLE FOR THE CHAIN, IS HAMMERED INTO SHAPE, SO THERE IS NO NEED FOR ANY SOLDERING.

1 Using a piercing saw, cut out a 4 cm (1½ in) square from the silver sheet. Round the corners and file the edges.

2 Hit the edges of the silver shape squarely and evenly with a hammer on a hard metal surface, rotating it to make an edge to contain the enamel. If you find it hard to work with, anneal the silver to soften it.

3 Drill a hole in one corner of the keyring to fit the silver tube. File the hole if necessary. Cut a small piece of tube to pass through the hole and protrude very slightly each side. Gently tap the ends with a hammer and punch to enlarge them.

4 Remove the oxidation from the silver. Grind and clean the grey-blue enamel then wet-apply it up to the edges of the keyring to make a base layer for the decoration. Fire and then repeat for the back.

5 Place the enamel threads on a plate and select the thick, straight ones. Using pliers, break them into short equal lengths. Cut the *cloisonné* wire into similar lengths with scissors.

6 Using a fine paintbrush dipped in enamel gum, arrange the threads and wire on the base enamel. When dry, fire gently until the decoration just fuses to the enamel base coat. Repeat for the back. Polish with pumice powder and water. Attach the fitting using a jump ring.

MATERIALS AND EQUIPMENT YOU WILL NEED

PIERCING SAW • 1.2 MM THICK SILVER SHEET • FILE • HAMMER • DRILL • SILVER TUBE • PUNCH • PICKLE SOLUTION (SEE BASIC TECHNIQUES) • PESTLE AND MORTAR • TRANSPARENT DARK GREY-BLUE ENAMEL • CONTAINER FOR ENAMEL • FINE ARTIST'S PAINTBRUSH • KILN AND FIRING EQUIPMENT • ENAMEL THREADS IN VARIOUS COLOURS • GLASS OR WHITE PLATE • SMALL, FLAT PLIERS • 0.5 MM ROUND SILVER *CLOISONNÉ* WIRE • SMALL, SHARP SCISSORS • ENAMEL GUM • PUMICE POWDER • KEYRING FITTING AND LARGE JUMP RING

GOLD FOIL BEADS

EMBELLISH A VARIETY OF ENAMELLED SILVER BEADS WITH TINY PIECES OF GOLD FOIL FOR A REALLY OPULENT EFFECT. INSTEAD OF A CHAIN, YOU COULD THREAD A FEW BEADS ON TO LEATHER THONGING OR A SILK CORD, AVAILABLE FROM BEAD SUPPLIERS, FOR A MORE UNUSUAL LOOK.

1 Assemble a collection of silver beads in different shapes and sizes to add interest to the necklace.

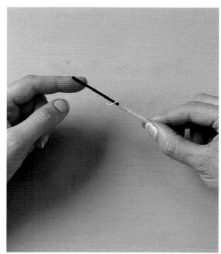

2 Cut a length of annealed round silver wire. Spiral it around a metal rod of the same thickness as the diameter of the holes in the beads.

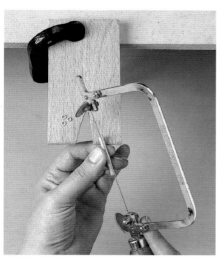

3 Remove the rod then cut down the length of the spiral, using a piercing saw, to make jump rings. Bend the rings to close the join and solder with hard solder. ▶

MATERIALS AND EQUIPMENT YOU WILL NEED

SELECTION OF SILVER BEADS • 1 MM ROUND SILVER WIRE • SCISSORS • METAL ROD, THE SAME DIAMETER AS THE HOLES IN THE BEADS •
PIERCING SAW • HARD SOLDER • SOLDERING EQUIPMENT • PLIERS • GLASS FIBRE BRUSH • MESH TRIVET • PESTLE AND MORTAR •
TURQUOISE TRANSPARENT ENAMEL • CONTAINER FOR ENAMEL • FINE ARTIST'S PAINTBRUSH OR QUILL • KILN AND FIRING EQUIPMENT •
DIAMOND-IMPREGNATED PAPER • GOLD FOIL • ENAMEL GUM • NAIL BUFFER • NECKLACE CHAIN • ASSORTED SILVER AND SEMI-PRECIOUS BEADS •
NECKLACE FINDINGS AND CLASPS • EASY SOLDER OR EPOXY RESIN GLUE

4 Using hard solder, solder the jump rings around the holes at the top and bottom of each bead. Remove the firestain and rinse, then clean the beads with a glass fibre brush and water.

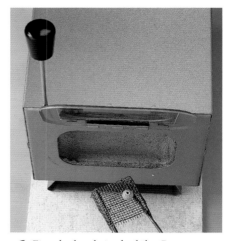

6 Fire the beads in the kiln. Repeat with two more layers of enamel, firing each layer. Abrade the enamel smooth with diamond-impregnated paper and water.

8 Polish the silver edges of the beads with a nail buffer. Thread on to the chain, mixing the enamelled beads with plain silver and semi-precious beads.

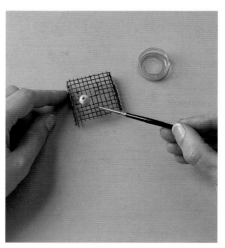

5 Cut and bend a piece of wire up from the trivet and place the bead on it to hold it during enamelling. Grind and clean the enamel then add a few drops of enamel gum and water to cover. Using the wet enamel as dry as possible, apply the enamel to the beads with a fine paintbrush or quill. Dry out the beads on top of the kiln.

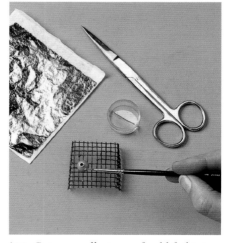

7 Cut up small pieces of gold foil into geometric shapes with sharp scissors. Attach them to some of the enamelled beads with a fine paintbrush dipped in a little enamel gum. Dry on top of the kiln then fire.

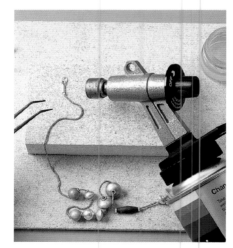

9 Attach the findings to the chain using easy solder. Solder or glue on a clasp. The clasp can be glued if using a leather or silk cord.

CLOISONNÉ BOWL

THIS BEAUTIFUL BOWL IS DECORATED WITH DELICATE WIRE MOTIFS THEN ENAMELLED IN BRIGHT COLOURS. A LAYER OF GOLD AND SILVER FOIL UNDER THE TRANSPARENT ENAMELS ADDS RICHNESS TO THE COLOURS. TO OFFSET THE ORNATE INTERIOR, THE BACK OF THE BOWL IS ENAMELLED IN PLAIN, DEEP BLUE.

1 Clean the back of the copper bowl with pumice powder and water, using a clean cloth.

2 Apply enamel gum over the back of the bowl with a wide paintbrush. Using a sieve, sift the 80-mesh royal blue enamel evenly over the top. Leave to dry then fire in the kiln. When cool, apply a second coat. Fire on a trivet. Clean the inside of the bowl and apply clear flux. Apply a second coat and fire. It is important to create a barrier of flux between the copper base and the silver. If they come into contact with each other there is a lowering of the melting point of the silver. This is called a 'eutectic' reaction.

3 Cut wide strips of silver foil with scissors. Using a fine paintbrush and enamel gum, lay the strips all over the inside of the bowl.

4 Using a sieve, sift the flux over the silver foil. Fire in the kiln. ▶

MATERIALS AND EQUIPMENT YOU WILL NEED

SMALL COPPER BOWL • PUMICE POWDER • CLEAN COTTON CLOTH • ENAMEL GUM • MEDIUM WIDE PAINTBRUSH • 80-MESH SIEVE AND SIEVE FOR GROUND ENAMELS • 80-MESH TRANSPARENT ROYAL BLUE ENAMEL • KILN AND FIRING EQUIPMENT • TRIVET • FLUX FOR SILVER • SILVER AND GOLD FOIL • SMALL, SHARP SCISSORS • FINE ARTIST'S PAINTBRUSH • SILVER AND GOLD CLOISONNÉ WIRE • SMALL PLIERS • PESTLE AND MORTAR • TRANSPARENT ENAMELS • CONTAINERS FOR ENAMELS • DIAMOND-IMPREGNATED PAPER • FILE • EPOXY RESIN GLUE • ROUGE • SMALL CIRCLES OF FELT

5 Cut lengths of silver and gold wire and bend into shapes with pliers. Place in position with enamel gum. Apply gold foil in the centre of the gold wire sun. Fire the wire shapes into the silver flux surface. Be careful not to overfire.

7 Fire and leave to cool, then re-apply the enamel colours and fire again. Gradually build up the layers to the top of the *cloisonné* wires: you will need about six layers.

9 Re-apply enamel where necessary and re-fire. Cut tiny squares, diamonds and triangles from silver wire. Using enamel gum, add to the design and fire. Remove the trivet by tapping gently. File the edges of the bowl to remove oxidation and any sharp edges left by the trivet. Polish with pumice powder and water and then rouge. Glue the felt circles to the base.

6 Grind and wash the enamels. Using a fine paintbrush, begin to wet apply the colours to the design.

8 Abrade the bowl with diamond-impregnated paper and water. Check that the wires are visible and clear of enamel.

BANDED RING

A CENTRAL BAND OF ENAMEL WITH A SIMPLE PHOTO-ETCHED DESIGN MAKES AN ELEGANT SILVER RING. YOU CAN OMIT THE FINAL FIRING IF YOU WOULD PREFER A MATT FINISH TO THE ENAMEL. TAKE GREAT CARE NOT TO OVERHEAT THE RING DURING FIRING IN CASE THE SOLDERED JOINT SPLITS OPEN.

1 Photocopy the template at the back of the book to produce a high contrast black-and-white design. This needs to be photo-etched on to the ring blank or silver sheet (see Basic Techniques section and Suppliers). Place in a clamp and shorten according to required finger size by filing the ends. File, then emery (sand) the sides.

2 Using pliers, bend in the ends to form a ring. It doesn't need to be perfectly round at this stage. File the ends of the ring so that they will meet exactly and make a good joint.

3 Twist binding wire around the ring. Solder the joint with hard solder, then quench in cold water and dry. Remove the wire, then pickle the ring.

4 File off excess solder. Place the ring on a ring mandrel and tap with a mallet until perfectly round. Remove firestain by placing in nitric acid, then rinse. Using a brass brush, brush with water and washing-up liquid (liquid soap) until shiny.

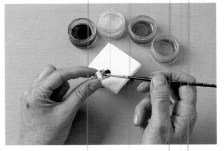

5 Grind and clean the enamels, then add a drop of enamel gum. Apply using a paintbrush or quill. Leave to dry, then fire in the kiln. Leave to cool.

6 Using medium-grade diamond-impregnated paper and water, abrade the enamel until you expose the silver design. Rinse and apply more enamel to the shiny areas then repeat the firing and abrading. Polish with fine-grade diamond-impregnated paper, rinse then fire again to glaze the surface. Leave to cool then pickle, rinse and polish the ring.

MATERIALS AND EQUIPMENT YOU WILL NEED

SILVER RING BLANK OR SILVER SHEET • RING CLAMP • FILE • EMERY PAPER (FINE SANDPAPER) • PLIERS • BINDING WIRE • SOLDERING EQUIPMENT • HARD SOLDER • PICKLE SOLUTION (SEE BASIC TECHNIQUES) • RING MANDREL • WOODEN OR LEATHER MALLET • NITRIC ACID • BRASS BRUSH • WASHING-UP LIQUID (LIQUID SOAP) • PESTLE AND MORTAR • TRANSPARENT ENAMELS • CONTAINERS • ENAMEL GUM • FINE ARTIST'S PAINTBRUSH OR QUILL • KILN AND FIRING EQUIPMENT • DIAMOND-IMPREGNATED PAPER • PUMICE POWDER OR FELT POLISHING MOP

STAR-PATTERNED BOX LID

A ROLLING MILL MAKES IT VERY SIMPLE TO TRANSFER DECORATIVE PATTERNS ON TO A PIECE OF METAL SUCH AS SILVER OR COPPER. INSTEAD OF SEQUIN WASTE, YOU COULD USE LACE, AN OPENWEAVE FABRIC OR A THICK WATERCOLOUR PAPER WITH CUT OUT STENCIL PATTERNS.

1 Place the sequin waste on top of the annealed silver sheet.

2 Adjust the rollers on the rolling mill so that, when the silver is run through the rolling mill, there is enough pressure to impress the sequin waste pattern on to the silver. Run them through the mill together.

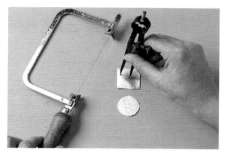

3 Using dividers, draw a circle on the reverse of the patterned silver slightly larger than the diameter of the silver box lid. Cut out with a piercing saw.

4 Anneal and pickle the silver. Then place in the doming block. Using a wooden punch and mallet, create a perfect dome shape by moving the silver round as you repeatedly tap the punch.

5 Using coarse emery paper (sand-paper), abrade the edges of the domed silver disc until they are flat.

6 Remove firestain and de-grease the silver disc, using a glass fibre brush and water. Always take care not to get any glass fibres into your hands. ▶

MATERIALS AND EQUIPMENT YOU WILL NEED

SEQUIN WASTE • 1 MM THICK SILVER SHEET • ROLLING MILL • DIVIDERS • SMALL ROUND SILVER BOX • PIERCING SAW • PICKLE SOLUTION • DOMING BLOCK • WOODEN DOMING PUNCH • MALLET • COARSE EMERY PAPER (SANDPAPER) • GLASS FIBRE BRUSH • HOUSEHOLD SCISSORS • 0.3 MM FINE SILVER *CLOISONNÉ* WIRE • ENAMEL GUM • PESTLE AND MORTAR • TRANSPARENT ENAMELS: SAPPHIRE BLUE, PALE TURQUOISE AND MID-TURQUOISE • CONTAINERS FOR ENAMELS • FINE ARTIST'S PAINTBRUSH OR QUILL • KILN AND FIRING EQUIPMENT • DIAMOND-IMPREGNATED PAPER • 'FINE' SILVER SETTING STRIP OR 'FINE' SILVER SHEET CUT INTO A STRIP 0.5 MM THICK, 5 MM (¼ IN) WIDE AND THE LENGTH OF THE CIRCUMFERENCE OF THE DOME • SOLDERING EQUIPMENT • HARD SOLDER • 1 MM ROUND SILVER WIRE • EASY SOLDER • BURNISHER • WET-AND-DRY PAPER • ROUGE AND FELT POLISHING MOP

7 Cut the required lengths of *cloisonné* wire and curve so that the wire fits to the dome and makes the geometric pattern. Position the wires with a fine brush dipped in enamel gum.

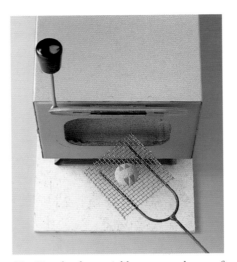

9 Fire the dome. Add two more layers of enamel, firing each layer. The enamel should now reach the top of the wire. Abrade the enamel flat with diamond-impregnated paper and water, clean with the glass fibre brush and water. Re-fire.

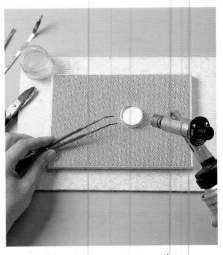

11 Solder the setting strip and its surrounding wire band into position on top of the silver box lid, using easy solder. Pickle and rinse.

8 Grind and clean the enamels and cover with water and a few drops of enamel gum. Using a fine paintbrush or a quill, apply a thin layer of wet enamel into the cells defined by the wire pattern.

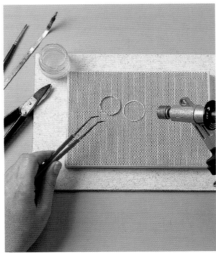

10 To make the setting, bend the setting strip to fit around the dome base. Cut to size and join the ends using hard solder. Repeat with the round wire, this time fitting to the outside of the setting.

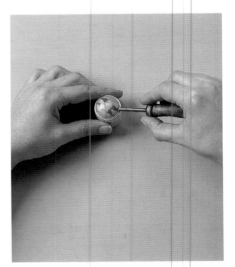

12 File the setting to be just high enough to trap the dome when set. Place the enamelled dome into its setting and push down gently with a burnisher. Polish the silver with successively finer grades of wet-and-dry paper. Finally polish with a rouge and a felt polishing mop.

CLOISONNÉ BROOCH

IN *CLOISONNÉ* WORK, FINE WIRES ARE LAID DOWN IN A PATTERN TO MAKE CELLS FOR THE ENAMEL COLOURS. HERE THE ENAMEL IS ALSO ENCLOSED WITHIN A WIRE RECTANGLE, WHICH ACTS AS A FRAME. THE BROOCH SHOWS HOW THIS TRADITIONAL TECHNIQUE PERFECTLY SUITS A MODERN DESIGN.

1 Cut two lengths of 1 mm square silver wire 5 cm (2 in) long. Holding a square needle file at an angle, file a triangular-shaped groove 18 mm (¾ in) from one end of both wires, through the thickness of the wires to a depth of approximately 0.8 mm. Anneal the wire, then bend to make a right angle. Solder the mitre with hard solder on both wires.

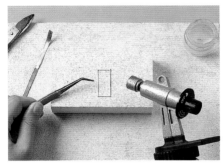

2 File the two L-shapes so that they will fit together and make a rectangular frame. Solder together with hard solder.

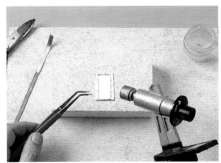

3 Place the wire rectangle on the silver sheet. Lay pieces of hard solder around the outside of the wire frame and solder it to the silver sheet. Cut off the excess silver sheet but do not file the edges until enamelling is complete.

4 Place the piece in a swage block, with the side to be enamelled face down. Using a wooden punch and mallet, create a curved shape. ▶

MATERIALS AND EQUIPMENT YOU WILL NEED

METAL SNIPS • 1 MM SQUARE SILVER WIRE • SQUARE NEEDLE FILE • SOLDERING EQUIPMENT • HARD SOLDER • 1 MM THICK SILVER SHEET • PIERCING SAW • SWAGE BLOCK • WOODEN DOMING PUNCH • MALLET • BROOCH FITTINGS • GLASS FIBRE BRUSH • 0.3 MM FINE SILVER *CLOISONNÉ* WIRE • SCISSORS • FINE ARTIST'S PAINTBRUSH • ENAMEL GUM • PESTLE AND MORTAR • TRANSPARENT ENAMELS: TURQUOISE, BLACK, GREY AND LIGHT AMBER • OPAQUE ENAMEL: BRIGHT RED • CONTAINERS FOR ENAMELS • QUILL (OPTIONAL) • TRIVET • KILN AND FIRING EQUIPMENT • DIAMOND-IMPREGNATED PAPER • GLASS FIBRE BRUSH • WET-AND-DRY PAPER • NAIL BUFFER

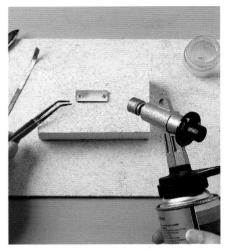

5 Solder the brooch fittings on the back, using hard solder.

6 Remove firestain and clean the front of the brooch thoroughly with a glass fibre brush and water. Cut the *cloisonné* wire into the required lengths and place on the brooch to make the geometric pattern, using a fine paintbrush dipped in enamel gum.

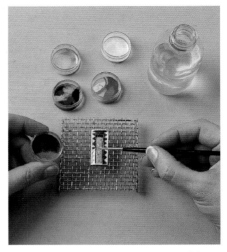

7 Grind and clean the enamels. Add a few drops of enamel gum to each colour and water to cover. Using a fine paintbrush or quill, apply the enamel to the cells between the *cloisonné* wires.

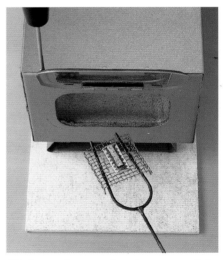

8 Leave the enamel to dry on top of the kiln, then fire. Apply two more layers of enamel, firing each layer. The enamel should now reach the top of the wire.

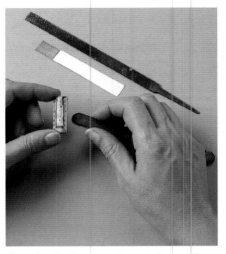

9 Abrade the enamel using diamond-impregnated paper and water until it is even, exposing any *cloisonné* wires that have been covered. Rinse thoroughly with a glass fibre brush and water and re-fire. File the outer edges of the brooch.

10 Clean and polish the edges of the silver with wet-and-dry paper and a nail buffer. Attach the brooch pin.

PLIQUE-À-JOUR EARRINGS

CREATE YOUR OWN DESIGN FOR THESE EARRINGS, USING PALE, CLEAR COLOURS THROUGH WHICH THE LIGHT CAN SHINE. THE HOLES IN YOUR DESIGN SHOULD BE LARGE ENOUGH TO ALLOW THE LIGHT TO SHOW THROUGH BUT SMALL ENOUGH TO HOLD THE WET ENAMEL.

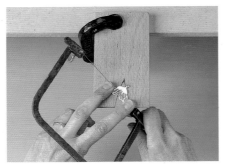

1 Draw your design on paper and attach it to the silver sheet. Using a piercing saw, cut out the shapes. Drill holes where the enamel will appear, then insert the saw into each hole and cut out. Use the saw to smooth the edges from front and back.

2 Shape the silver with tweezers. Clean the silver with a brass brush and washing-up liquid (liquid soap) solution. Grind and wash the transparent enamels.

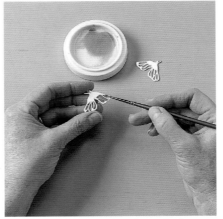

3 Using a fine paintbrush, apply the wet enamel into the spaces in the earrings. Practise getting the right consistency – if the enamel is too wet, it will fall through.

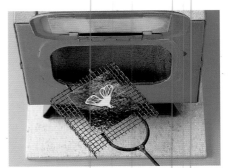

4 Fire while the enamel is still damp. Beginners may find it easier to fire on a sheet of mica. Remove as soon as the enamel begins to melt. Refill the holes if the enamel has pulled to the side and re-fire.

5 When the holes are completely filled, abrade the earrings with diamond-impregnated paper. Rinse and fire again. Polish with pumice powder and water, then rouge. Attach the wires.

MATERIALS AND EQUIPMENT YOU WILL NEED

PENCIL AND PAPER • 1.2 MM THICK SILVER SHEET • PIERCING SAW • DRILL • TWEEZERS • BRASS BRUSH •
WASHING-UP LIQUID (LIQUID SOAP) SOLUTION • PESTLE AND MORTAR • TRANSPARENT ENAMELS IN PALE COLOURS •
CONTAINERS FOR ENAMELS • FINE ARTIST'S PAINTBRUSH • TRIVET • KILN AND FIRING EQUIPMENT • SHEET OF MICA (OPTIONAL) •
DIAMOND-IMPREGNATED PAPER • PUMICE POWDER • ROUGE • EARRING WIRES

FISHY CUFFLINKS

CHOOSE TRANSPARENT ENAMELS IN WATERY COLOURS FOR THESE FISH, SET AGAINST A DEEP BLUE SEA IN LUSTROUS SILVER FRAMES. WHEN THE DESIGN IS PHOTO-ETCHED, MAKE SURE IT IS REVERSED FOR THE SECOND BLANK SO THAT THE CUFFLINKS MAKE A SYMMETRICAL PAIR.

1 Photocopy the template at the back of the book to produce a high contrast black-and-white design. This needs to be photo-etched on to the cufflink blanks or silver sheet. Cut out the cufflink shapes with a piercing saw, then place each one in a clamp and file the edges straight. Polish the edges using a fine emery stick (board).

2 Place each cufflink into the doming block. Tap with a doming punch and mallet to create the desired domed shape.

3 De-oxidize the earrings by placing in nitric acid for a few minutes and then rinsing in cold water. Using a brass brush, scrub with washing-up liquid (liquid soap) solution until the metal is shiny.

4 Grind and clean the enamels and add a drop of enamel gum to each. Apply the wet enamels, using a paintbrush. Do not mix the colours. Let dry, then fire in the kiln until molten. Leave to cool.

5 Using medium-grade diamond-impregnated paper and water, abrade the enamel to expose the silver design and rinse. Apply more enamel and repeat. Polish with fine-grade paper, then fire again. Leave to cool. Remove the oxidation with emery paper (fine sandpaper).

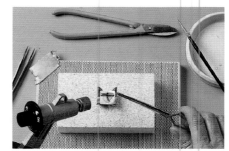

6 Melt easy solder on to the foot of each finding and solder to the back of the cufflink. Cool, then pickle and polish.

MATERIALS AND EQUIPMENT YOU WILL NEED

SILVER CUFFLINK BLANKS, TO FIT THE TEMPLATE, OR 1.1 MM THICK SILVER SHEET • PNP BLUE ACETATE FILM AND IRON (IF USED) • PIERCING SAW • RING CLAMP • FILE • EMERY STICK (BOARD) • WOODEN DOMING BLOCK • WOODEN DOMING PUNCH • MALLET • NITRIC ACID • BRASS BRUSH • WASHING-UP LIQUID (LIQUID SOAP) SOLUTION • PESTLE AND MORTAR • TRANSPARENT ENAMELS • CONTAINERS FOR ENAMELS • ENAMEL GUM • FINE ARTIST'S PAINTBRUSH OR QUILL • TRIVET • KILN AND FIRING EQUIPMENT • DIAMOND-IMPREGNATED PAPER • EMERY PAPER (FINE SANDPAPER) • SOLDERING EQUIPMENT • EASY SOLDER • CUFFLINK FINDINGS • PICKLE SOLUTION • PUMICE POWDER OR FELT POLISHING MOP (OPTIONAL)

TRIANGULAR PENDANT

CREATE YOUR OWN *CHAMPLEVÉ* DESIGN TO FIT WITHIN THIS ELEGANT SHAPE, REMINISCENT OF ART DECO JEWELLERY. THE PENDANT ILLUSTRATED HAS SOME *CLOISONNÉ* DETAILING AND IS 5 CM (2 IN) LONG AND 2 CM (¾ IN) WIDE AT THE TOP. USE THE ENAMEL COLOURS LISTED HERE OR CHOOSE YOUR OWN.

1 Trace template 1 from the back of the book on to tracing paper. Attach the tracing to the thinner silver sheet with double-sided tape.

2 Cut out the outer shape with a piercing saw. Drill holes inside the shape to allow access for the saw blade and cut out the inner design. File and smooth the inside edges.

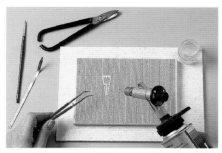

3 Melt some small pieces of hard solder on to the back of the pierced-out pendant shape.

4 Place the pierced-out sheet, solder side down, on the thicker silver sheet. Place hard solder around the outside and solder the pierced shape to the sheet. If any solder runs into the areas to be enamelled, it must be removed.

5 Following template 2, saw off the excess silver sheet, leaving a tab at the top for a loop and a circle at the bottom. Do not file the edges. Drill a hole in the centre of both tab and circle.

6 Place the pendant face down in a swage block. Using the doming punch on its side, tap it into a curved shape using a mallet.

▶

MATERIALS AND EQUIPMENT YOU WILL NEED

TRACING PAPER AND PENCIL • RULER • 0.5 MM THICK SILVER SHEET • DOUBLE-SIDED TAPE • PIERCING SAW • DRILL • FILE •
SOLDERING EQUIPMENT • HARD SOLDER • 1 MM THICK SILVER SHEET, CUT SLIGHTLY LARGER THAN THE PENDANT TEMPLATE •
SWAGE BLOCK • WOODEN DOMING PUNCH • MALLET • DOMING BLOCK • SILVER CHAIN • GLASS FIBRE BRUSH • TRIVET • SMALL, SHARP SCISSORS •
0.3 MM FINE SILVER *CLOISONNÉ* WIRE • FINE ARTIST'S PAINTBRUSH • ENAMEL GUM • PESTLE AND MORTAR • TRANSPARENT ENAMELS: TURQUOISE,
LIGHT AMBER, BRIGHT BLUE AND GREY • CONTAINERS FOR ENAMELS • QUILL (OPTIONAL) • KILN AND FIRING EQUIPMENT •
DIAMOND-IMPREGNATED PAPER • WET-AND-DRY PAPER • NAIL BUFFER • CLASP

7 Cut out a circle of silver sheet fractionally larger than the circle at the bottom of the pendant. Place in a doming block and create a small dome. File the base of the dome flat.

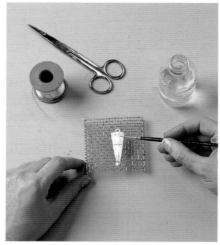

9 Cut the required lengths of *cloisonné* wire and place into the recesses in the pendant in a geometric pattern, using a fine paintbrush dipped in enamel gum.

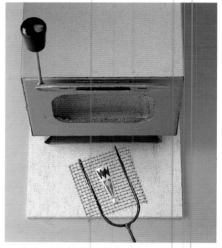

11 Leave the enamel to dry on top of the kiln, then fire. Apply two more thin layers of enamel, firing each time.

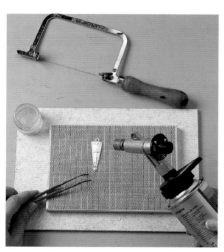

8 Solder the dome on to the circle at the bottom of the pendant with hard solder. Use a piercing saw to make the opening in the tab large enough to take your silver chain. Clean the metal with a glass fibre brush and water. Place on a trivet.

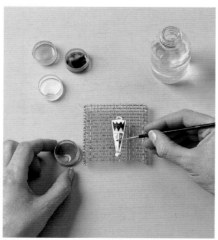

10 Grind and clean the enamels. Add a few drops of enamel gum and water to cover. Apply the enamel to the cells, using a fine paintbrush or quill.

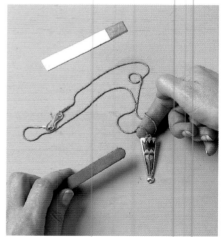

12 Abrade the enamel with diamond-impregnated paper and water. Clean with a glass fibre brush and water. Re-fire. File the silver edges of the pendant. File the surface silver flush with the enamel or leave it raised. Smooth the silver areas with wet-and-dry paper and finish with a buffer. Thread the chain through the loop. Solder on a clasp and polish.

REPTILIAN RING

T HE SUBTLE DESIGN RESEMBLING SNAKESKIN ON THE TOP OF THIS HANDSOME RING IS ETCHED AND THEN ENAMELLED IN TWO SHADES OF GREY. ENGRAVE A MATCHING DESIGN AROUND THE EDGE OF THE RING. THE DIMENSIONS GIVEN HERE WILL MAKE A MEDIUM TO LARGE RING.

1 Using ½ round-nosed pliers, bend the strip of 2 mm thick silver into a ring smaller than the finger size. Solder the joint, using hard solder. Pickle and rinse.

2 Check the ring is a circle by placing it on the mandrel and correcting it with a mallet. File, then sandpaper inside and out.

3 File the sides parallel. Scribe a light centre guideline around the outside. With the joint at the top, file a taper on both sides from a width of 8.5 mm (⅜ in) at the bottom to 4 mm (³⁄₁₆ in) at the top. Engrave a reptilian design around the outside, using a graver. The design can also be acid-etched.

4 For the top, place the 17 mm diameter annealed silver into the doming block. Using a doming punch and a mallet, tap into a hemispherical shape.

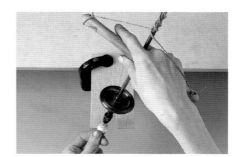

5 Drill a 1 mm hole in the centre of the domed top. ▶

MATERIALS AND EQUIPMENT YOU WILL NEED

½ ROUND-NOSED PLIERS • STRIP OF 2 MM THICK SILVER, 8.5 MM (⅜ IN) WIDE AND 5.8 CM (2¼ IN) LONG, FOR THE RING • SOLDERING EQUIPMENT • HARD SOLDER • PICKLE SOLUTION • RING MANDREL • MALLET • FILE • EMERY PAPER (FINE SANDPAPER) • GRAVER • CIRCLE OF 1 MM THICK SILVER, 17 MM DIAMETER, FOR THE DOMED TOP • DOMING BLOCK • DOMING PUNCH • DRILL • STRIP OF 1.5 MM THICK SILVER, 2 MM WIDE AND 6 CM (2½ IN) LONG, FOR THE BEZEL • CIRCLE OF 1 MM SILVER, 2 CM DIAMETER, FOR THE BASE • 4 MM (³⁄₁₆ IN) SQUARE OF 0.6 MM THICK SILVER • 14BA ³⁄₁₆TH CHEESEHEAD BRASS SCREW AND MATCHING NUT • STOPPING-OUT VARNISH • FINE ARTIST'S PAINTBRUSH OR QUILL • NITRIC ACID • CONTAINER FOR ACID • GLASS FIBRE BRUSH • BRUSH CLEANER • BRASS BRUSH • WASHING-UP LIQUID (LIQUID SOAP) SOLUTION • EASY SOLDER • PUMICE POWDER • TOOTHBRUSH • PESTLE AND MORTAR • TRANSPARENT ENAMELS: MID-GREY AND DARK GREY • CONTAINERS FOR ENAMELS • KILN AND FIRING EQUIPMENT • CARBORUNDUM STONE OR DIAMOND FILE • WET-AND-DRY PAPER • EPOXY RESIN GLUE

6 Using the ½ round-nosed pliers, bend the strip of 1.5 mm silver into a collar, or bezel, to fit snugly around the base of the domed top. Solder the joint with hard solder. Check the shape is a circle on the ring mandrel, as before.

7 Solder the 2 cm (¾ in) diameter circle of silver to the bezel with hard solder to make the base. File the edge of the base flush with the bezel, then file both to create an angled profile.

Drill a 1 mm hole through the centre of the 4 mm (³⁄₁₆ in) silver square, then dome it to match the top. Thread the brass screw through the hole from the top and secure with hard solder underneath. File the top of the screw to make a decorative feature.

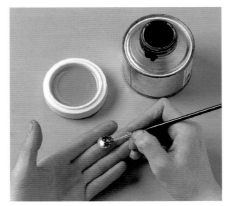

8 Clean and de-grease the silver. Apply stopping-out varnish to the back, edges and hole of the domed top. Leave to dry, then paint a reptilian design in varnish on the front. Place in 1 part nitric acid: 3 parts water for 3–3½ hours until the design is etched to a depth of 0.1– 0.2 mm. Rinse, using water and a glass fibre brush, then remove any remaining varnish with brush cleaner. Brighten the top with a brass brush and washing-up liquid (liquid soap) solution.

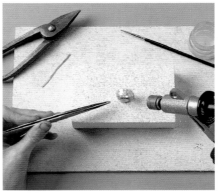

9 Solder the bezel to the narrowest point of the ring strip at the joint, using easy solder. File and sand then apply pumice powder with a toothbrush, followed by a glass fibre brush and washing-up liquid (liquid soap) solution.

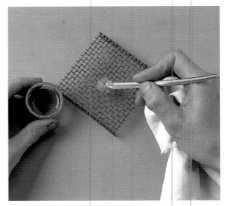

10 Grind and clean the enamels. Wet-apply the mid-grey enamel to the entire top surface, checking that it does not run into the hole. Fire in the kiln and leave to cool. On the next three to four layers, emphasize the etched recesses with dark-grey enamel to suggest scales. Use mid-grey for the rest of the design.

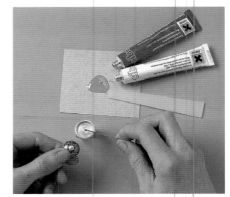

11 Use a carborundum stone or diamond file and wet-and-dry paper, to abrade the enamel. Use a glass fibre brush to rinse under running water, then fire for the final time. When cool, scrub with a slurry (paste) of pumice powder and a toothbrush. Thread the decorative feature through the central hole of the dome and secure using the 14BA nut. Glue into the bezel using epoxy resin glue.

FLOWER PENDANT

DECORATE THE PENDANT WITH AS MANY ENAMEL COLOURS AS YOU LIKE, INCLUDING SEVERAL SHADES OF GREEN, TO RECREATE THE EFFECT OF A SUMMER GARDEN IN FULL BLOOM. THE DESIGN IS PHOTO-ETCHED ON TO THE SILVER READY FOR ENAMELLING.

1 Photocopy the template at the back of the book. Photo-etch the design on to the pendant blank or silver sheet. Cut out the shape with a piercing saw and file the edges until circular, then sand.

3 Grind and clean the enamels, then add a drop of enamel gum. Apply the wet enamels, using a paintbrush or quill. Take care not to mix the colours. Leave to dry, then fire in the kiln. Leave to cool.

5 Leave to cool, then remove the oxidation from the back of the pendant with emery paper (fine sandpaper).

6 Bend the wire into a loop and melt easy solder on to the ends. To attach the loop to the pendant, hold the loop in tweezers against the back of the pendant and heat the ends until they join. Leave to cool, then pickle and polish the pendant as desired.

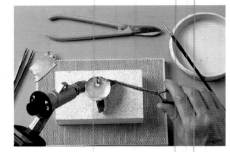

2 Shape the pendant in a doming block, using a doming punch and mallet. Place in nitric acid for a few minutes, then rinse with water. Scrub the pendant with a brass brush and washing-up liquid (liquid soap) solution.

4 Using diamond-impregnated paper and water, abrade the enamel to expose the silver design, then rinse. Apply more enamel to the shiny areas, then repeat. Abrade and fire again.

MATERIALS AND EQUIPMENT YOU WILL NEED

SILVER PENDANT BLANK, TO FIT THE TEMPLATE, OR 1.1 MM THICK SILVER SHEET • PnP BLUE ACETATE FILM AND IRON (IF USED) • PIERCING SAW • RING CLAMP • FILE • EMERY STICK (BOARD) • WOODEN DOMING BLOCK • WOODEN DOMING PUNCH • MALLET • NITRIC ACID • BRASS BRUSH • WASHING-UP LIQUID (LIQUID SOAP) • PESTLE AND MORTAR • TRANSPARENT ENAMELS • CONTAINERS FOR ENAMELS • ENAMEL GUM • FINE ARTIST'S PAINTBRUSH OR QUILL • TRIVET • KILN AND FIRING EQUIPMENT • DIAMOND-IMPREGNATED PAPER • FINE-GRADE EMERY PAPER (SANDPAPER) • SMALL PIECE OF SILVER WIRE • EASY SOLDER • SOLDERING EQUIPMENT • TWEEZERS • PICKLE SOLUTION • PUMICE POWDER OR FELT POLISHING MOP (OPTIONAL)

CLOISONNÉ EARRINGS

D ECORATE THESE RECTANGULAR EARRINGS WITH YOUR OWN *CLOISONNÉ* DESIGN. HERE, THE ENAMELLED TRIANGLES ECHO THE OUTLINE OF THE SILVER MOUNTS. SMALL SHAPES FASHIONED FROM SILVER WIRE ADD A FINAL FLOURISH. USE THE ENAMEL COLOURS LISTED HERE OR CHOOSE YOUR OWN.

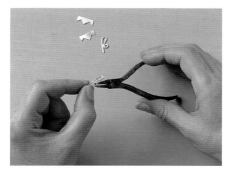

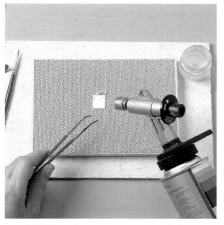

1 Cut two rectangles 16 x 22 mm (⅝ x ⅞ in) from the thicker silver sheet. To create the earring tops, trace template 1 from the back of the book on to tracing paper. Attach to the thinner silver sheet with double-sided tape. Cut out twice, using a piercing saw.

2 File and smooth the edges of the two cut-out earring tops with a fine emery stick (board). Cut two lengths of round silver wire and bend into matching shapes with pliers – see template 2 for shape.

3 Melt hard solder on to the back of the earring tops and the straight part of the wire design.

4 Position the earring tops and the wire designs, solder side down in place on top of the silver rectangles. Flux the metal and rerun the solder with the blowtorch. ▶

MATERIALS AND EQUIPMENT YOU WILL NEED

PIERCING SAW • 1 MM THICK SILVER SHEET • TRACING PAPER AND PENCIL • 0.5 MM THICK SILVER SHEET • DOUBLE-SIDED TAPE • FILE • FINE EMERY STICK (BOARD) • METAL SNIPS • 1.2 MM ROUND SILVER WIRE • PLIERS • SOLDERING EQUIPMENT • HARD SOLDER • SWAGE BLOCK • WOODEN DOMING PUNCH • MALLET • SILVER EARRING FINDINGS • BURNISHER • GLASS FIBRE BRUSH • SCISSORS • 0.3 MM FINE SILVER *CLOISONNÉ* WIRE • FINE ARTIST'S PAINTBRUSH • ENAMEL GUM • TRIVET • PESTLE AND MORTAR • TRANSPARENT ENAMELS: TURQUOISE, LIGHT AMBER, BRIGHT BLUE • CONTAINERS FOR ENAMELS • QUILL (OPTIONAL) • KILN AND FIRING EQUIPMENT • DIAMOND-IMPREGNATED PAPER • WET-AND-DRY PAPER • NAIL BUFFER

5 Place each earring face down in a swage block. Lay a wooden doming punch along its length and tap with a mallet to create a curved shape.

7 Cut the required lengths of *cloisonné* wire and lay on each earring in a geometric pattern, using a fine paintbrush dipped in a little enamel gum. Place on a trivet.

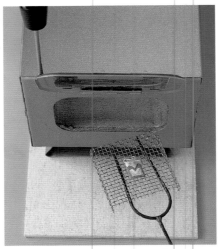

9 Allow to dry on top of the kiln, then fire. Apply two more layers of enamel, firing twice more. The enamel should now reach the top of the wire.

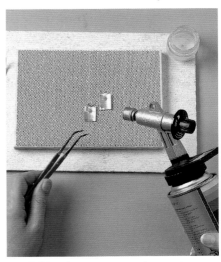

6 Solder the earposts to the earrings with hard solder. Burnish the edges of the earrings to provide a 'grip' for the enamel to adhere to. Clean the metal with a glass fibre brush and water.

8 Grind and clean the enamels. Add a few drops of enamel gum and cover with water. Using a fine paintbrush or quill, apply the enamel to the 'cells' between the *cloisonné* wires.

10 Abrade the enamel with diamond-impregnated paper and water to expose any *cloisonné* wire that may have been covered. Rinse and re-fire. Smooth the silver with wet-and-dry paper and finish with a buffer.

MOON BOWL

*E*N *GRISAILLE* IS A VERY EARLY TECHNIQUE FOR PAINTING WITH ENAMELS IN WHICH A MONOTONE THREE-DIMENSIONAL IMAGE IS BUILT UP WITH THIN LAYERS OF OPAQUE WHITE ENAMEL. FOR THE FINAL FIRING, THIS MOON FACE IS DECORATED WITH SMALL STRIPS OF GOLD AND SILVER FOIL.

1 Clean the back of the bowl thoroughly with pumice powder and water, using a clean cloth.

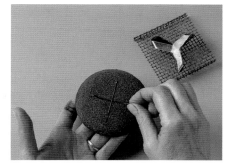

3 Place a trivet on the centre of the base. Fire the base a second time to fire the trivet in place. Clean the inside of the bowl without dislodging the trivet, then apply black enamel as on the back. Fire in an upright position.

5 Using a blunt tool, such as the end of an artist's paintbrush, scratch a moon face (or other design of your choice) through the white enamel.

2 Apply enamel gum over the back of the bowl with a medium-wide paintbrush. Using a sieve, apply the black enamel evenly over the top. Leave to dry, then fire in the kiln. When cool, apply a second coat in the same way.

4 Using a medium-wide paintbrush, apply enamel gum over the inside of the bowl. Gently sift white *grisaille* enamel over the top.

6 Remove the white enamel from the areas of the design you wish to appear black. Fire the bowl and leave to cool. ▶

MATERIALS AND EQUIPMENT YOU WILL NEED

SHALLOW COPPER BOWL • PUMICE POWDER • CLEAN COTTON CLOTH • ENAMEL GUM • MEDIUM-WIDE PAINTBRUSH • SIEVE • OPAQUE BLACK ENAMEL • KILN AND FIRING EQUIPMENT • TRIVET • OPAQUE WHITE 200-MESH *GRISAILLE* ENAMEL • FINE ARTIST'S PAINTBRUSH • PLATE • SMALL, SHARP SCISSORS • SILVER AND GOLD FOIL • FILE • EPOXY RESIN GLUE • SMALL CIRCLES OF FELT

7 Mix a thin paste of enamel gum and *grisaille* white enamel on a plate. Using a fine paintbrush, accentuate the main areas of the design to make them appear prominent.

9 Cut small strips of silver and gold foil with scissors. Using a fine paintbrush moistened with enamel gum, pick up the foil pieces and place them in rings around the moon face.

10 Fire the bowl for the final time, then remove the trivet by tapping gently. File the edges of the bowl to remove oxidation and smooth any sharp edges left by the trivet.

8 Fire again. Leave to cool, then repeat the thin application of enamel up to 12 times to create the desired effect.

11 Glue small felt circles to the base to enable the bowl to stand on a polished surface.

WAVE BROOCH

THIS MODERN BROOCH IS MADE IN THREE LAYERS, COPPER SANDWICHED BETWEEN TWO PIECES OF SILVER. THE DESIGN IS ACCENTUATED BY STENCIL-ROLLED WAVES ON ONE PIECE OF SILVER BEFORE ENAMELLING, WHICH CREATES A TEXTURED EFFECT.

1 Cut the watercolour paper larger than the piece of 1 mm silver sheet. Draw stylized wave shapes on the paper and cut out carefully with a craft knife to make a stencil.

2 Anneal the 1 mm thick silver sheet. Then remove firestain by placing it in nitric acid until it appears white. Place the paper stencil on top of the silver sheet. Run them together through the rolling mill, with the rollers tightly clamped down. Emphasize the waves by engraving a few lines around them with a graver.

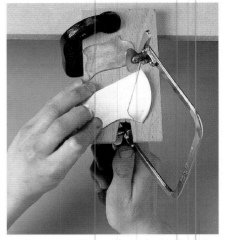

3 Trace template 1 from the back of the book on to the copper sheet and cut out with a piercing saw. Using a scriber, draw round this shape on to the 0.8 mm silver sheet. Cut out the silver just outside the marked line so that it is slightly larger than the copper.

MATERIALS AND EQUIPMENT YOU WILL NEED

SCISSORS • ROUGH-TEXTURED WATERCOLOUR PAPER • 1 MM THICK SILVER SHEET, 4 X 2.5 CM (1½ X 1 IN) • PENCIL • CRAFT KNIFE • NITRIC ACID • ROLLING MILL • GRAVER • TRACING PAPER • SCRIBER • 1 MM THICK COPPER SHEET, 4 X 6 CM (1½ X 2½ IN) • PIERCING SAW • 0.8 MM THICK SILVER SHEET, 4 X 6 CM (1½ X 2½ IN) • FILE • DRILL • FOUR 14BA ³⁄₁₆TH CHEESEHEAD BRASS BOLTS AND MATCHING HEXAGONAL NUTS • BURNISHER • GLASS-FIBRE BRUSH • WASHING-UP LIQUID (LIQUID SOAP) SOLUTION • PESTLE AND MORTAR • TRANSPARENT ENAMELS: TURQUOISE AND BLUE • FLUX • CONTAINERS FOR ENAMELS • FINE ARTIST'S PAINTBRUSH OR QUILL • TRIVET • KILN AND FIRING EQUIPMENT • CARBORUNDUM STONE OR DIAMOND FILE • WET-AND-DRY PAPER • PUMICE POWDER • TOOTHBRUSH • STOPPING-OUT VARNISH • BRUSH CLEANER • SOLDERING EQUIPMENT • HARD SOLDER • BROOCH FITTINGS • PICKLE SOLUTION

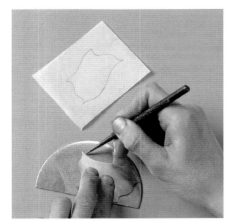

4 Trace template 2 on to the rolled silver and cut out. File the edges of all the pieces.

5 Drill a small hole in each corner of the rolled silver, to fit the brass screws. Burnish the edges to provide a lip to contain the enamel. Scrub with a glass fibre brush and washing-up liquid (liquid soap) solution, then rinse.

6 Grind and clean the enamels. Wet-apply the turquoise enamel, using a paintbrush or quill. Make sure it does not flow into the holes. Fire this first layer.

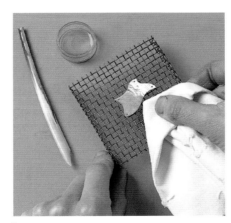

7 For the next three to four layers of enamel, emphasize the wavy lines by shadowing with blue and highlighting them with the flux, applied with a clean, dry cloth.

8 Abrade the fired enamel using a carborundum stone or diamond file, rinse, fill in low spots and re-fire if necessary. Abrade again followed by wet-and-dry paper, then scrub with a glass fibre brush under running water. Scrub back and sides with a slurry (paste) of pumice powder, using a toothbrush.

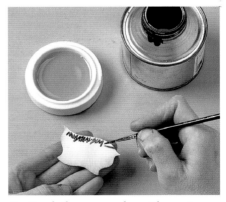

9 Scrub the copper also with pumice powder, then de-grease with a glass fibre brush and washing-up liquid (liquid soap) solution. Paint stopping-out varnish on the back and edges, and a 'breezy' border on the front. When dry, place in 1 part nitric acid: 3 parts water for about 5 minutes. Rinse, then remove any varnish with brush cleaner. File the edges. ▶

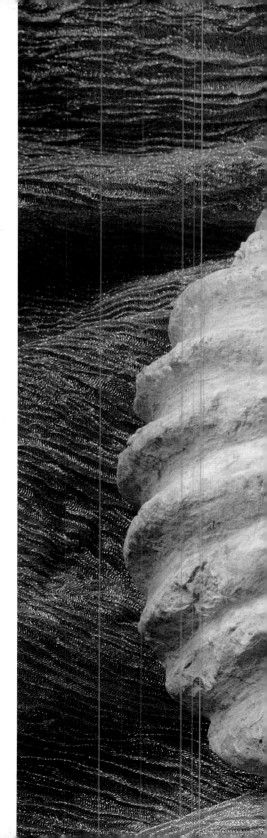

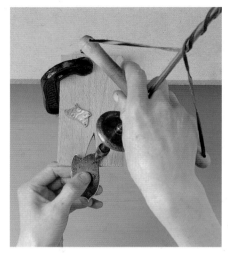

10 Gently shape the silver and copper backing pieces to match the curve of the enamelled piece. Colour the copper iridescent purple by gently heating it with a blowtorch. Drill holes in both pieces to match the enamelled piece.

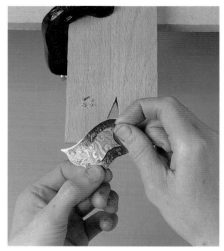

12 Clean with a glass fibre brush and washing up liquid (liquid soap) solution. Rivet the brooch pin. Assemble the brooch using brass screws and nuts.

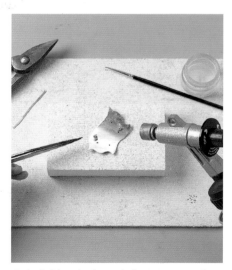

11 Solder the brooch fittings on to the backing piece using hard solder. Pickle and rinse. Abrade thoroughly with wet-and-dry paper, then with a toothbrush and a slurry (paste) of pumice powder.

Templates

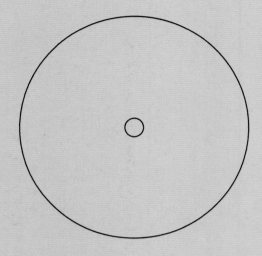

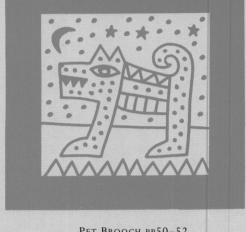

Pet Brooch pp50–52

Night and Day Clock Face pp45–47

Shield Earrings pp53–55

Fishy Cufflinks pp74–75

1

2

Wave Brooch pp90–93

Banded Ring pp64–65

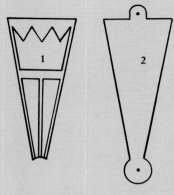

TRIANGULAR PENDANT PP76–78

FLEUR-DE-LIS BOOKMARK PP28–29

CLOISONNÉ EARRINGS PP84–86

FLOWER PENDANT PP82–83

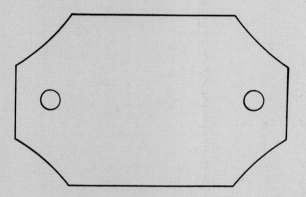

DOOR PLAQUE PP30–31

BIRD PIN PP40–41

STARGAZER EARRINGS PP34–36

SUPPLIERS

UNITED KINGDOM
Camden Workshops
84 Camden Mews
London NW1 9BX
Kilns and enamelling tools

Changs
43 Fulham High Street
London SW6 3JJ
Jewellery beads

Chempix
Bullock Street
Nechells
Birmingham B7 4DY
Tel: (0121) 359 5623
Photo-etchers

Cookson Precious Metals Ltd
43 Hatton Garden
London EC1N 8EE
Tel: (0171) 400 6500
Bullion findings

H J Edwards & Sons
93–95 Barr Street
Birmingham B19 3DE
Tel: (0121) 554 9041
Non-ferrous metals

Hogg Laboratory Supplies Ltd
Sloane Street
Birmingham B1 3BW
Chemical supplies

J Smith & Sons Ltd
42–56 Tottenham Road
London N1 4BZ
Tel: (0171) 253 1277
Non-ferrous metals

Kernowcraft
Bolingey
Perranporth
Cornwall TR6 0DH
Tel: (01872) 573 888
Findings and tools

Kilns & Furnaces
Keele Street Works, Tunstall
Stoke-on-Trent ST6 5AS
Tel: (01782) 813 621

Milton Bridge Ceramic
Colours Ltd
Unit 9, Trent Trading Park
Botteslow Street, Hanley
Stoke-on-Trent ST1 3NA
Enamels and kilns

The Enamel Shop
PO Box No 43
London SE19 2PN
Tel: (0181) 325 7272
Enamels and kilns

UNITED STATES
Art Cove Ltd
60–09 Myrtle Avenue
Ridgewood
NY 11385
Tel: (718) 381 7782

Dick Blick
PO Box 1267
Galesburg
IL 61402
Tel: (800) 828 4548

Goodman's Lumber
445 Bayshore Boulevard
San Francisco
CA 94124
Tel: (415) 285 2800

AUSTRALIA AND NEW ZEALAND
A and E Metal Merchants
Suite 59
104 Bathurst Street
Sydney 2000
Tel: (02) 9264 5211
Non-ferrous Metals

Dean's Art
188 Gertrude Street
Fitzroy Victoria 3065
Tel: (03) 9419 6633
Kilns and enamelling tools

*For further information contact
NSW Enamellers Association:
(02) 9918 6878 or (043) 415277*

INDEX